Benjamin M.

Earning Your

First Million

With The

Divide and Conquer

Strategy

Introduction

This book presents an in-depth account of an experimental strategy I developed for achieving financial goals through systematic saving and investing, or I called it the "Divide and Conquer" strategy. The approach began with a modest objective: saving enough money to purchase a brand new gaming laptop. I had just graduated from college at that time. Having a powerful gaming laptop was a dream for me, not just for personal work but entertainment as well. It took about 6 months for me to achieve it using this strategy.

Once this initial goal was accomplished, I scaled up the strategy to acquire increasingly expensive items, culminating in the ambitious target of saving $1 million. In this narrative, I will detail the entire process of this experiment, including the methods employed, the obstacles encountered, and the eventual results.

The primary aim of this book is to share the lessons learnt and insights gained from my personal journey. It is important to emphasise that this approach does not guarantee success for everyone, as results can vary significantly based on individual circumstances, environmental factors, and the element of luck. The effectiveness of this strategy can be influenced by a multitude of variables unique to each person's situation.

Therefore, throughout this journey, it is crucial to keep meticulous records of what strategies and actions yield positive results and which do not. By doing so, one can make informed adjustments and improvements to the approach. Success is often a product of learning from past mistakes and continuously refining one's strategy based on real-world feedback. This book aims to provide practical guidance and reflections that can assist readers in navigating their own financial goals, emphasising the importance of adaptability and perseverance in the pursuit of success.

Disclaimer

I do not offer investment classes or courses to the public. I am just merely sharing my knowledge and my story via this book. Therefore, this book should serve as just a reference and additional knowledge for you to formulate your own financial strategy according to your needs.

How did it start?

For many, it is a common expectation that when pursuing a significant financial milestone, such as saving up a large sum of money for a major purchase, e.g., a car or a dream house, one would work diligently to accumulate funds as rapidly as possible to achieve that target. While this approach is certainly valid and proven to be achievable, it is simply taking far too long by depending on savings alone. I tried searching for different strategies, combining the idea of passive incomes to drive up my income and increase my savings in order to achieve my goals faster.

In the formative years of my investment journey, I encountered several costly mistakes that underscored the critical need for ample capital. These early missteps highlighted the importance of having sufficient resources to manage cash flow effectively and to average down the price of shares. This was essential not only to mitigate potential losses but also to maximise opportunities for turning paper losses into profitable gains. The experience taught me that having a solid financial foundation was crucial for making informed and strategic investment decisions.

After a few trials and errors, burning thousands of dollars in the process, I recognised the importance of developing a systematic and disciplined saving strategy. My initial focus was on creating a method to accumulate capital efficiently. I started with a modest target: saving $10,000 for reinvestment into my stock portfolio. Through careful planning and a dedicated approach, I managed to achieve this goal in less than three months. This success provided a strong foundation for refining my strategy and applying it to increasingly ambitious financial objectives.

Encouraged by the results I achieved from this strategy, I expanded my goal to save for a more significant purchase: a brand-new car priced at $25,000. By employing the same systematic approach, I was able to reach this target in less than six months. This accomplishment was not only a testament to the effectiveness of my saving strategy but also a clear indication of the potential for scaling up my efforts.

Building on these successes, I set my sights on an even more ambitious challenge: saving $1 million. This goal represented a substantial leap from my previous targets and required an enhanced version of my saving strategy, along with a greater commitment of time and resources. Throughout this book, I will provide a detailed account of the evolution of my saving strategy, including the processes I implemented, the obstacles I faced, and the insights I gained along the way. By sharing this journey, I hope to offer valuable lessons and practical guidance for others who seek to achieve significant financial goals through disciplined saving and strategic investment.

Stage 1 : The First Step

To embark on the first step of your saving strategy, it is essential to equip yourself with the right tools to effectively plan and track your progress. You can opt for a computer that comes with the pre-installed spreadsheet application, which provides a highly efficient and organised way to monitor your savings, manage your budget, and adjust your plan as needed. Spreadsheets provide features such as automatic calculations, data visualisation, and ease of updating information, all of which streamline the tracking process and save significant time.

Alternatively, you might choose to use traditional methods like pen and paper to record your financial data, if that is your preference. I have friends who stick by the traditional pen-and-paper method when they want to record their thoughts or ideas. While this approach is straightforward and does not require digital tools, it can be more cumbersome when it comes to calculations and formulas. Tracking progress manually on paper can be less efficient and may involve additional costs for buying notebooks or sketchbooks, a move that is going against our goal. Moreover, paper records can be prone to errors and require more time to update and analyse.

If using a computer or digital tools is not an option and paper is your only resource, start by setting a clear goal, such as saving enough to purchase a laptop, so you may achieve better results in the long run and avoid wastage. Even with the limitations of paper, you can still make progress, but be mindful of the potential challenges. Nonetheless, investing in the proper tools, whether digital or otherwise, can greatly enhance your efficiency and effectiveness, ultimately freeing up more time for other aspects of your life and helping you achieve your financial objectives more smoothly.

Tools that you will need to start your journey:
- Computer with the spreadsheet function, e.g., Excel
- Pen and paper or a sketchbook

- A healthy mindset with the can-do spirit and never afraid to fail countless times in your journey

Stage 2 : The Next Step

Once you have prepared enough, both mentally and physically, I mean having the tools, not hitting the gym, the next step in implementing your saving strategy is to determine the amount you wish to save and the timeframe for achieving your goal. The best thing about the strategy is that you have total control and freedom to choose the strategy and adjust the formula that works for you. However, before you start diving into action, it is crucial to assess your current financial situation, skills, and income sources to ensure that your goal is both achievable and realistic. Setting an unattainable goal will undermine the effectiveness of your plan, as you would be aware from the outset that it is beyond your reach.

To create a realistic and motivating goal, consider the following factors: your present financial situation, including your income and expenses; your skills and how they can be leveraged to increase your earnings; and any additional income streams you may have. A positive mindset is essential throughout this process, as the journey toward your goal will require consistent effort and will be more rewarding with regular milestones.

For example, as a recent graduate with a starting salary of $2,000 per month as a junior web developer, you might set an initial savings target of $10,000. With your skills in web development and graphic design, you can explore additional income opportunities such as freelance projects, designing websites, or creating graphics for clients. Your hobbies, such as photography and handicrafts, might also offer potential avenues for generating extra income, whether through selling prints or handmade items.

Once you achieve your first goal of saving $10,000, set a new, higher target. This progressive approach will keep you challenged and motivated, as each new goal should build upon the previous one. By consistently increasing your savings targets, you can continue to grow your financial reserves and tackle more ambitious objectives over time. The key to success is maintaining a clear focus on your goals, regularly evaluating your progress, and adapting your strategy as needed to overcome any obstacles and achieve greater financial milestones.

Getting started - Step 1

Step 1: Open up the Excel spreadsheet or set down your pen and paper.
Step 2: Set your goal
Step 3: Set a fixed amount of cells, or a set of boxes.
Step 4: Set a value for each box.

Goal: A new, powerful gaming laptop
Target: $ 2,000
Total cells: 20

100	100	100	100
100	100	100	100

100	100	100	100
100	100	100	100
100	100	100	100

Are you following so far? Great!

Next, you will need to list out your current income stream(s). For example,

- Job as a junior web developer
- Freelance graphic design work

Next, list down your hobbies or other skill sets that you think you can monetise. Using the example given previously, you would have the following skills.

- Photography
- Creating handicrafts

Tips: Do not worry if you currently do not have adequate skills or hobbies that you can start monetising. I would recommend that you do some soul searching to find out what your passions and interests in life are. You may start trying out those things, like photography, design, etc., and you will know immediately. If things go well for you, you might even be able to create your own business with the skills you have obtained throughout the journey.

Once you have all the items listed, take out your calculator or open the calculator app to prepare for some calculations.

Getting started - Step 2

In the example given previously, I have divided the cells or boxes into $100 each for an easy start. You can set your own target according to your needs or capabilities.

Next, take your gross salary and deduct your monthly expenses that include your rent, food, and bills. You may set aside some amount of money for your wants and leisure if so desired. But in this example, I will be using the extreme case, where you will live off just your needs and not your wants.

Let's say after deducting all your expenses, you are left with 500 dollars left.

Take the $500 and cross out 5 boxes/cells from your 100 boxes/cells. Congratulations! You have achieved 25% of your target.

Goal: A new, powerful gaming laptop
Target: $ 2,000 (500/2,000)
Total cells: 5/20
Progress: 25%

100	100	100	100
100	100	100	100
100	100	100	100
100	100	100	100

| 100 | 100 | 100 | 100 |

If you continue to set aside $500 every month, you will achieve your goal in 4 months time. You realised that you just got paid another $500 this month for your freelancing work. You have no use for the money for the moment, even though spending it at a nice, fancy restaurant seems like a good idea after all the hard work. If you choose to save it up, you will have another 25% completed.

Goal: A new, powerful gaming laptop
Target: $ 2,000 (1,000/2,000)
Total cells: 10/20
Progress: 50%

100	100	100	100
100	100	100	100
100	100	100	100
100	100	100	100
100	100	100	100

If you continue to make $500 every month from your freelancing work and save up $500 from your salary, then you will achieve your target in just 2 months time. If you manage to earn more from your freelancing work, then you will be able to reach your goal faster.

Comparison,

1. If just relying on just your monthly salary > Time to reach your target: 4 months
2. Your monthly salary and your freelancing work > Time to reach your target: 2 months

But you are still not satisfied with having to wait 2 months for it. What can you do?

You remembered that you have great photography skills, where you could use them to make some extra cash. However, you lacked the professional tools to produce the high-quality photos. You needed a high-quality DSLR camera to produce outstanding work for your clients. Getting one now will set you back or even land you in debt if your savings are not sufficient. You are tempted to swipe that credit card, but is that a good option? Do you need to get more debts?

Whenever I have some wants, like the brand new iPhone, I would take a look at my table. Do I really want to take away the green spots and take more time to complete the table? Or I can make do with whatever I have to achieve my goals. Sure, if you wish to create better work, you will need better tools for it. However, it is important to know your limits and adjust your saving strategy to accommodate additional expenditure so it will not derail or put a stop to your momentum.

So what can you do about it in this dilemma?

Goal: A new, powerful gaming laptop
Target: $ 2,000 (1,000/2,000)
Total cells: 10/20
Progress: 50%

100	100	100	100
100	100	100	100
100	100	100	100
100	100	100	100
100	100	100	100

I am an impatient person, and I wanted to complete the table and reach my goal and use it for my purchase as planned. If you have multiple income streams or have an increased income from promotion or bonuses, you could do it concurrently, which I will show later on. However, if you have a change of heart, you can always change your goal to something else. One of the benefits of saving through this strategy is that it will help prevent you from making impulsive purchases, which would just waste your hard-earned money on something that you might not even need. It has happened to me countless times where I lost the urge or desire after a few weeks. On the plus side, I have some extra cash lying around for me to plan out something else.

Tips: Avoid impulsive purchases at all costs. You can list down your wish list and check back again after a week to see if you still want that item. Weigh in the pros and cons before making the purchase. Your purchase should always bring value or benefit to your life and not screw you up!

Let's go back to the original scenario. You are able to strike off 10 boxes/cells per month. Now you are able to utilise your photography skills to earn some extra income. At this stage it is up to you to be creative in thinking of new ways to make money. You accepted that you are not able to afford the DSLR camera at this stage, but you have a decent camera, and you have a friend that owns a DSLR camera.

You could,

- Use your own camera for now, and touch up later using graphic editing tools to enhance the photo quality.
- You could borrow the DSR camera from your friend, for free or at a cost (by leasing).
- Or if your friend is also doing freelance photography, you may approach him to collaborate together on your projects, with a predetermined profit-sharing ratio.

After deciding on a plan, you can include photography services as part of your freelancing offering. Let's say you started off with lacklustre results, but you are still able to generate $100 for your work. That is another box to strike off. If you are able to generate more income over the next months, you will be able to strike off more boxes.

Month 1: 10 boxes - **$1,000**

Month 2 (with added income from the photography services): 11 boxes - **$1,100**

Month 3 (more income from your photography services): 15 boxes - **$1,500**

In just 3 months, you are able to save up $3,600, compared to $3,000 if you are saving only using your income. That is about 20% extra to your savings plan.

If you continue to build momentum in the photography work, then you will be about to create another goal for your DSLR camera.

Goal: A new, powerful gaming laptop
Target: $ 2,000 (1,500/2,000)
Total cells: 15/20
Progress: 75%

100	100	100	100
100	100	100	100
100	100	100	100
100	100	100	100
100	100	100	100

Goal: My dream DSLR
Target: $ 3,000 (0/3,000)
Total cells: 0/30

Progress: 0%

100	100	100	100	100	100
100	100	100	100	100	100
100	100	100	100	100	100
100	100	100	100	100	100
100	100	100	100	100	100

Tips: Remember, you are free to switch your goals at any given point and adjust your saving plan at any given time. Just keep up the momentum and increase the amount to continue the progress!

What if I have an emergency?

If you encounter an emergency that requires you to access the funds you've saved, it's permissible to withdraw the money and replenish it later or adjust your target timeframe to accommodate the unforeseen circumstances. However, it's crucial to avoid making this a frequent practice. Consistently dipping into your savings for nonessential reasons can undermine your progress and lead to frustration, making it more challenging to stay motivated and achieve your goal.

Our brains are motivated by seeing tangible progress, and frequent setbacks or slow advancement can diminish our drive. Maintaining a clear focus on your objectives and observing even small improvements can provide the encouragement needed to keep moving forward. Each step forward, no matter how minor, contributes to building momentum and reinforcing your commitment to reaching your financial targets. By adhering to your plan and reserving withdrawals for true emergencies, you can maintain a steady path towards your goal, ensuring that your motivation remains high and your progress continues to build effectively.

Tips: Remember to always replenish back the amount that you have spent for emergencies if you are capable, so you can get back on track towards achieving your goal.

Stage 2 : Growing your money

Assuming that you have completed the first stage successfully, where you have saved up $10,000 in total. You are wondering what you can do with this amount of money. Rather than wasting it on modern gadgets or useless luxury goods that benefit nothing but your ego, you plan to utilise the money to grow it even further.

The "Divide and Conquer" strategy is a flexible method that you can use to meet your objectives. Think of the strategy as a game where you will unlock additional skills as you move up to the next level. This comes together with the amount of money that you will be able to get more and save more.

Let's continue with the scenario given previously with the best outcome. After a year following through with the strategy and plan, you are able to improve on your skills and gain new experience at your workplace and also your freelancing job. You are able to expand your freelancing business with the onboarding of additional clients, and you are considering having a business partner or another person to help you out.

Originally, your main income sources were

- Job as a junior web developer
- Freelance graphic design work
- Photography work

You have received a promotion at work, and now your new salary is adjusted to $2,500. You are able to make $1,000 per month now from your freelancing work as you get more clients or recurring projects from your existing clients. You still get $500 per month extra from the photography service that you provide.

With that, let's do some calculations.

- Job as a junior web developer - $2,500
- Freelance graphic design work - $1,000
- Photography work - $500

That is $4,000 per month. Let's say your expenses remain the same. With your new salary, you are now able to save up $1,000 (500 from the original savings and now with the extra $500).

Net saving income: $1,000 + $1,000 + $500 = $2,500

With this figure, you will be able to create another pile of $10,000 in about 4 months, compared to the initial 10 months if you are saving around $1,000 per month. But we want to constantly challenge ourselves. It makes life more fun, unless you are satisfied with the status quo and don't mind maintaining the current pace;

then you can continue with it. But you will notice that it will take you a shorter period every year to save up to $10,000.

If you are up for the challenge, you will now set a higher target. You increase your goal to $25,000. With this, you will roughly need about 10 months to reach your goal. However, this time you have more tools at your disposal. You have the $10,000 that you have saved up previously, or whatever is left after your expenditure.

So what can you do with the $10,000 savings?

Remember you have the hobby of making handicrafts? Maybe you can use some of the money to purchase the material required for you to produce some of the handicraft work for sale. If I have the extra $10,000. I would place it in a high-interest fixed-term deposit. Let's take it at 5% per annum for easy calculation. With savings, you would have roughly $41.67 return on interest. If you leave it there, you would get the following:

Note: The table below is only used for reference and not a definite guide for your saving growth. The returns depend on the interest rate given by your bank in your country.

Month	Interest	Accrued Interest	Balance
0	–	–	$10,000.00
1	$41.67	$41.67	$10,041.67
2	$41.84	$83.51	$10,083.51

3	$42.01	$125.52	$10,125.52
4	$42.19	$167.71	$10,167.71
5	$42.37	$210.08	$10,210.08
6	$42.54	$252.62	$10,252.62
7	$42.72	$295.34	$10,295.34
8	$42.90	$338.24	$10,338.24
9	$43.08	$381.31	$10,381.31
10	$43.26	$424.57	$10,424.57
11	$43.44	$468.00	$10,468.00
12	$43.62	$511.62	$10,511.62

Disclaimer: The table above is for illustration only; the rate of return is subject to the rate set by the bank.

In a year, you would make an extra $511.62 from the interest with your $10,000 deposit.

Let's take the 10-month period and assume that you managed to meet your objective set for this round as well.

So now, you will have the following after a 12-month period:

- Box 1 - initial $10,000 + interests after a 12-month period $10,511.62

Savings of Year 2 at $2,500 per month

- Box 2 - $10,000 from 4 months of savings at $2,500 per month + 4 months of interest in fixed-term Term savings $10,167.71

- Box 3: $10,000 from 4 months of savings at $2,500 per month + 4 months of interest in fixed-term savings $10,167.71

- Box 4 - Box 3 $10,000 from 4 months of savings at $2,500 per month + 4 months of interest in fixed-term savings $10,167.71

By the third year, you would have approximately **$41,014.75** as a capital for your next saving or investment plan.

Tips: I would recommend you save up most of the money as an emergency fund or a baseline for a minimum savings amount before you embark on your next step in your investment journey or even start your own business. This minimum amount is to serve as a safety net, where you will be able to recover faster if you experience any slump later on. Furthermore, having this practice actually helps you to prepare better mentally, as you won't be easily tempted with the latest gadget or trend that would be a financial disaster or wastage for you. Plus, your mental state about your finances will be healthier, knowing that you have a backup that you can dip into whenever there is a financial crisis.

You continued to make progress in your career, but your freelancing work is stagnant due to spending more time at your main job. You gave more commitment to your job and were promoted to a team lead in your third year of work. The new role comes with a salary of $3,000.

In the third round, you would have the following cash and assets:

Saving Pot	Current Amount	Usage Plan
1	$10,511.62	Long Term Saving
2	$10,167.71	Lifestyle Expenditure
3	$10,167.71	Saving for a home down
4	$10,167.71	Emergency Fund

For easier management, label your saving pots according to your needs. This will allow you to keep track of your available funds for different purposes and avoid overspending, as the amount will act as the max limit that you should be spending without touching the funds for other purposes. Otherwise, you would be derailing all your hard work and effort thus far. Personally, I would set aside about **$50,000** as my long-term savings (high yield/returns) and **$10,000** for my emergency fund as the baseline when I am still having a recurring income stream to protect myself from any unexpected events or unavoidable circumstances, e.g., layoffs, medical emergencies, etc., where I can dig into my funds without encountering any cash flow issues or disrupting other investment plans that are in motion.

Saving Pot	Current Amount	Usage Plan

1	$50,000.00	Long Term Saving
2	$10,000.00	Emergency Fund
3	<set target amount>	Stock investment
4	<set target amount>	House downpayment

The table is just for your reference. You may customise your saving pots according to your needs. Each saving pot will be your own individual goal. You can start growing your saving pots according to your budget based on your income stream.

Let's go back to your daily job.

- Job as a junior web developer - $2,500
- Freelance graphic design work - $1,000
- Photography work - $500

In the third year, let's say you got promoted to the team lead position, and your salary is adjusted to the following.

- Job as Lead Web Developer - $3,500
- Freelance graphic design work - $1,000
- Photography work - $500

Your expenses increased $1,000 a month because you have decided to treat yourself better. You have **$4,000** left to allocate to your saving pots.

Stage 3 - Diversification and Expansion

Amount	Saving Pot 1 (Long Term)	Saving Pot 2 (Emergency Fund)	Saving Pot 3 (Investment)
50,000			
50,000			
40,000			
30,000			
20,000			
10,000			?

Illustration: You may create the diagram above to monitor your goals for each specific saving pot.

Once you have gotten the hang of the process in stage 2, it is time to take up the challenge and create the multi-income streams in a more complex setup. In this chapter, we will be discussing how you can create multiple passive incomes using the same method that you have mastered in stage 2.

Let's look at the original setup that we have in stage 2.

- Job as Lead Web Developer - $3,500
- Freelance graphic design work - $1,000
- Photography work - $500

These are considered active incomes where you will need to put in effort, time, and resources every day to get the compensation. If you stop the activity for the period of time or completely, then your income stream would be reduced or stopped entirely as well. In order to reach our goal within the period of time that we have set, or even earlier, we will have to make every dollar count. Hence, we will need to start looking into passive income.

Definition of Passive Income from Investopedia, Passive Income." Investopedia, https://www.investopedia.com/terms/p/passiveincome.asp.

Passive income *refers to earnings generated with little to no effort on the part of the recipient. It often involves investments that produce regular income, such as rental properties, dividends from stocks, or interest from savings accounts. Unlike active income, which requires continuous work (like a salary or hourly wage), passive income can flow in without ongoing active involvement.*
Having good passive income is crucial to help you reach your goals faster since you will be able to generate passive income even when you are sleeping. You are free to focus on your active income stream, increase the monthly contribution to the passive income pool, and reinvest any earnings through the dividend income back. Through the power of compounding, you will soon find your passive income saving pots increase tremendously over a period of time.

Types of passive incomes include:

- **Dividend Stocks**: Stocks that pay dividends allow you to earn money without having to sell the shares.

- **Real Estate Investments**: Renting out properties can provide a steady stream of income, especially if you use property management services.

- **High-Interest Savings Accounts**: Some savings accounts offer interest that can generate passive income over time.

- **Royalties from Creative Works**: If you create art, music, or writing, you can earn royalties whenever your work is sold or used.

- **Create an Online Course**: Once created, an online course can continue to sell and generate income with minimal ongoing effort.

- **Affiliate Marketing**: Earning commissions by promoting other people's products through your website or social media can provide passive income.

- **Investing in REITs**: Real Estate Investment Trusts allow you to invest in real estate without having to manage properties directly.

- **Bond Investments**: Bonds pay interest over time, providing a regular income stream.

- **Automated Business Models**: E-commerce stores that use drop shipping or print-on-demand can generate income with little ongoing effort.

For your day job and freelancing work, we will label them as **Active Income**. Next we will create that **Passive Income** label for your next income. You are free to create as many labels as you want to fit your liking and income generation strategy. The basic idea here is to have multiple income generators to increase the amount of money.

The strategy that I employed was setting up and categorising the passive income saving pots into the following based on my capabilities at that time:

1. Stock dividend income for the long term
2. Royalties (I did product photography and artworks to be sold online and to some graphic designers, where I get paid if they used my artwork for their projects, and from my eBooks sold online)
3. Rental incomes, including REITs investment income

Advice: Avoid overstretching your budget allocation and resources into the passive income savings pot, as it is better to establish a stable, recurring passive income before focusing on the next passive income with your limited resources. In the military strategy, it is a bad thing to stretch your supplies thin. The same strategy applies to your financial strategy, as the last thing we want to do is to disrupt our progress in the mid to long term.

At this point, you have an estimated **$41,014.75** in savings from the progress in the previous round. During the last 10 months, you have decided to brush up on your knowledge on investments. I wouldn't advise anyone to jump into the stock market directly with the meagre extra cash without first understanding the fundamentals and developing a strategy using the demo accounts. For more tips on investments, you can look around many great books and websites online for free. I would advise against signing up for the courses offered by those so-called investment gurus. They would most probably make more money selling courses than their investments.

Investment is easy. You will only need a few things: common sense, no FOMO (Fear Of Missing Out attitude), and a focus goal of increasing the value of your asset and cash flow.

I would offer the same advice to anyone asking me for investment advice: just make money, not lose it. Your step is always aiming for the positive. There is no get-rich scheme, just accumulation and watching your wealth grow over the years if you are consistent and avoid greed.

Alright, back to the progress,

The third round is what I called a turning point. It could either go badly, or it could give a huge boost to your goal. For me, at this round I took the leap and set my new target to $1 million. But of course you could set it to $50,000 or $100,000 before increasing it progressively to 1 million. I was impatient, not because of greed, but I like to make it a challenge for myself. Having said that, this round was vastly different from the previous two rounds. In the previous rounds, you would set a fixed duration to reach your target. However, in the third round, we are setting $1,000,000 as our target. Anyone who said you can reach it in 10 months is either delusional, crazy, or lucky enough to strike a lottery, or even win the jackpot at the casino.

For the third round, your plan should focus on creating as many income streams as possible to strike off as many boxes/cells as possible within the shortest period of time.

Goal: Stock investment
Target: $ 10,000
Total cells: 20 ($500 per month allocated)
Progress: 0%

500	500	500	500
500	500	500	500
500	500	500	500
500	500	500	500
500	500	500	500

As you have learnt in the previous chapters, you can create another goal for yourself and set aside some money consistently to reach that goal. Here, we will set the goal to **$10,000** for investments with a return of about 7 to 8 percent.

If you are able to set aside additional money, for example, using your 1-month bonus of $2,000, then you will be able to see the growth happen at a faster rate.

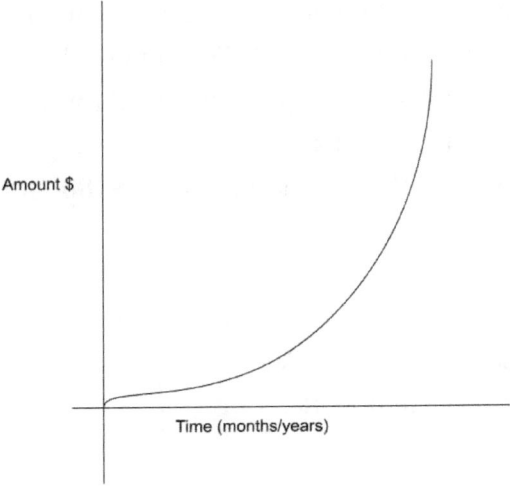

Your investment growth should follow an exponential path as illustrated above. However, any investment comes with a risk. Therefore, you will need to constantly balance your portfolio and sell off the assets or stocks to increase that pile of cash. You should forgo the attitude of, "The price of the stock or the value of the asset will go up further." While it might be true, the price could come down, usually at a faster rate. The best way to invest is to sell when there is a profit and purchase it back if you feel like that is a good stock to hold or focus on other undervalued stocks that will make you profits.

Other income stream ideas

You may opt for writing ebooks or creating handicrafts, or you may expand your freelance work into a full-time or side business or invest in companies as a shareholder.

I once did a garage sale with items collected from family and friends and made a total profit of **$1500**, minus the cost and expenditure. The sale went so well that it became a weekly thing, as I could sell my handicrafts that I made during my free time during the garage sale as well, and that brought in **$1000** for me.

Going back to our setting,

- Job as a web developer - team lead
- Freelance graphic design work
- Photography work

You could organise a garage sale and start your own merchandise business, selling T-shirts and other merchandise through your graphic design skills at the sales. You could get some friends to replicate the garage sales in their neighbourhoods and sell your merchandise through those sales as well. If things are going very well, you could rake in a handsome profit that can be used as capital for your investments or other ventures.

For example, you can sell off the business for **$100,000** because sales are starting to dwindle, while still profitable. Businesses can be assets that can be sold off for profit if you time it right.

Tips: Having a progression chart greatly helps in giving you the motivation to pursue your intended goals. The chart will also provide insight on what went well and what didn't so you may adjust your strategy accordingly.

Keep An Eye on Your Debt

Debt can significantly impact our daily lives in both subtle and obvious ways, affecting everything from our financial stability to our emotional well-being. Having bad debts accrued could easily wipe out our progress and waste our effort that we have put in to save up the money. In short, bad debt will cause:

1. Financial Strain and Cash Flow

When you have outstanding debt, a portion of your income is often tied up in monthly payments. Whether it's credit card bills, student loans, or a mortgage, this ongoing obligation limits your disposable income, which can affect your ability to cover other essentials like food, utilities, transportation, or even savings. If the debt is large or the interest rates are high, it can feel like you're constantly treading water, struggling to keep up.

For example, if your debt payments consume a significant chunk of your pay cheque, you may have less money available for things like leisure activities, home improvements, or unexpected expenses, making day-to-day life feel more stressful.

2. Psychological and Emotional Toll

Debt can have a significant psychological impact. Constant worry about bills, creditors, and falling behind can cause anxiety, stress, and even depression. The pressure of owing money can affect sleep, concentration, and relationships, leading to feelings of shame or failure, even if the debt was incurred through necessary means like medical expenses or education.

This mental burden can also result in poor decision-making or avoidance. People may procrastinate paying their bills or avoid opening mail, hoping the problem will disappear on its own. But, of course, this usually only worsens the situation.

3. Impact on Opportunities and Freedom

Debt can limit your freedom to make important life decisions. For example, if you're burdened with student loans, you may delay purchasing a home, starting a family, or pursuing other opportunities because you don't feel financially secure enough to take those steps. High debt can also hinder your ability to save for the future or invest in your long-term goals, such as retirement or starting your own business.

Additionally, carrying too much debt can affect your credit score, which in turn impacts your ability to get approved for loans or secure favourable terms on mortgages or car loans. It can also influence things like renting an apartment, getting a job (some employers check credit histories), or even buying insurance.

4. Interest Accumulation and Debt Growth

The longer you carry debt, especially high-interest debt like credit cards or payday loans, the more it grows. Interest payments can quickly compound, making it harder to pay down the principal balance. A small loan that seemed manageable can quickly escalate if interest keeps piling up. This can lead to a vicious cycle where more and more of your income goes toward servicing the debt, leaving less for other essential needs.

For example, if you have a credit card balance with an interest rate of 20%, and you only make the minimum payment each month, the balance will take much longer to pay off, and you'll end up paying far more than the original amount.

5. Impact on Relationships

Debt can also strain relationships, especially if it's shared or one person is responsible for it. Financial stress is one of the leading causes of conflict in relationships, whether it's a romantic partnership, family dynamics, or friendships. Disagreements may arise over how to manage or pay down the debt, or resentment can build if one person feels unfairly burdened by the financial responsibilities.

6. Debt Collection and Legal Consequences

If debt is left unpaid for too long, creditors can take more aggressive steps, including sending your account to collections, which can result in harassing phone calls, wage garnishment, or even legal action. This can cause significant stress and disruption to your daily life, as you may face constant reminders of your financial struggles or even the risk of losing assets like your home or car.

7. Behavioural Impact and Coping Mechanisms

In some cases, individuals might turn to unhealthy coping mechanisms when dealing with debt, such as excessive spending to "comfort" themselves or resorting to risky loans to try to consolidate or cover existing debt. This can create a pattern of behaviour that deepens the financial hole over time.

By staying aware of your debt, including the total amount you owe, the interest rates, and the due dates, you can make informed decisions about how to manage it. Keeping track allows you to prioritise payments, avoid late fees, and seek help if the debt becomes overwhelming. It also helps you create a strategy to pay off high-interest debt first or consolidate multiple debts into a more manageable payment.

Being proactive about debt helps maintain your financial health and reduces the long-term stress and damage that can come from letting debt accumulate. It gives you more control over your finances and enables you to move toward financial freedom, instead of being constantly burdened by the weight of unpaid bills and looming obligations.

Amount	Saving Pot 1 (Long Term) Savings)	Saving Pot 2 (Emergency)	Loans
50,000			
50,000			
40,000			
30,000			■
20,000			■
10,000			■

Illustration: You can use the same method to track your savings as you do with monitoring your debt. Assign different colours, such as green for positive balances and red for amounts owed. Your goal is to increase the green section while reducing the red to zero.

If you understand the basic concepts of saving pots and how to create them to reach your goals, then you are ready to move on to the core idea of what this book is about: using the "Divide and Conquer" strategy to reach your financial goal.

Life as a Battlefield

Imagine for a moment that your journey towards financial success, towards that first million, is not a leisurely walk in the park. Instead, picture it as a challenging, yet ultimately rewarding, campaign waged on a vast and complex battlefield. This is your financial battlefield, and you are the commanding general, responsible for the fate of your financial future.

On this battlefield, your resources are not bullets and bombs, but your hard-earned money. Every dollar you earn, every penny you save, is a vital resource to be deployed strategically. How you manage these resources will determine whether you emerge victorious or fall in defeat. Every financial decision you make, big or small, is like a tactical command issued to your troops. Some decisions will lead you closer to your objective, strengthening your position and expanding your territory. Others might lead to setbacks, weakening your forces and leaving you vulnerable to attack. You will need to constantly make decisions and improve your decision-making.

This is not a game of chance, where victory is determined by a lucky roll of the dice. This is a game of skill, strategy, and discipline, where knowledge is your most powerful weapon. There are rules to learn, tactics to master, and enemies to overcome. But there are also allies you can recruit, opportunities you can seize, and ultimately, victory that you can achieve.

The most important thing to understand is that you are in command. You are the general, the strategist, the decision-maker.

Your choices will determine the outcome of this battle. You have the power to shape your financial destiny.

In this financial war, your savings are your loyal and dedicated troops. They are your financial army, ready to be deployed to the battlefield. We call them your "saving pots." Each pot represents a different division of your army, each trained and equipped for a specific purpose. You might have a pot for emergencies, another for long-term goals like buying a house, and yet another for seizing investment opportunities. These saving pots are the very foundation of your financial strength, and in previous chapters we have discussed how to amass these armies.

But your battlefield is not empty, nor is it a safe haven. It is occupied by opponents, represented by your debts. And just like any army, your opponents come in different forms, with varying levels of threat. Some debts are like treacherous landmines, hidden beneath the surface, waiting to detonate and inflict serious damage on your financial well-being. They are dangerous traps that will cost you time, money, and effort to recover. These are your "bad debts," and they are your primary enemy. They must be avoided at all costs.

However, not all debts are created equal. Some debts are like strategic strongholds or fortresses. At first glance, they might appear to be enemy territory, occupied and fortified against you. But, if you can conquer them through careful planning and the strategic deployment of your saving pots, they can be transformed into valuable assets. These strongholds, once captured, can generate income, provide strategic advantages, and help you secure victory on the battlefield. These are your "good debts," and they can be powerful allies if used wisely. Once you have conquered these fortresses, they will become your outposts, where you can oversee the surrounding area and plan your next move.

The key to winning this financial battle lies in your ability to distinguish between good and bad debt. You must learn to deploy your saving pots strategically, like a seasoned general manoeuvring their troops. And you must master the art of turning debt to your advantage, transforming potential liabilities into income-generating assets. You will also need to defend your empire to prevent any surprise attack from the enemies.

Just like a skilled general studies the battlefield, learns their enemy's strengths and weaknesses, and formulates a comprehensive battle plan, you must approach your finances with the same level of diligence and foresight. You need to plan your moves carefully, anticipate your opponent's actions, and always be prepared to adapt to changing circumstances. You need to constantly train your troops and improve your weapons; in this case, you will need to constantly improve your financial knowledge. The more you learn about the intricacies of this financial battlefield, the better equipped you will be to make informed decisions, outmanoeuvre your opponents, and secure your financial future.

In the following sections, we will delve deeper into the specifics of this battlefield. You will learn how to identify the different types of debt that exist, how to strategically deploy your saving pots to conquer those valuable strongholds, and how to build a solid and resilient financial foundation that will ultimately lead you to victory, to that coveted first million. We will also learn the mindset of a winner, a successful general, how to plan your move and strategy, and how to adapt to changes on the battlefield.

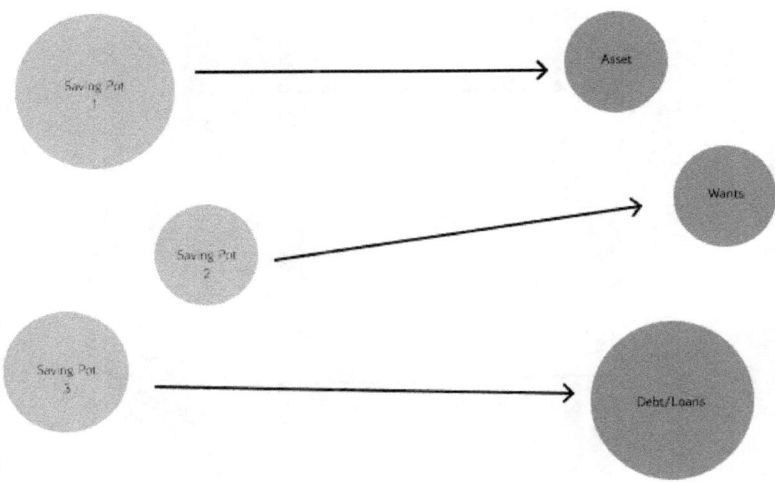

The normal scenario: you use respective saving pot for a specific goal, e.g a saving pot to save up for a laptop (wants)

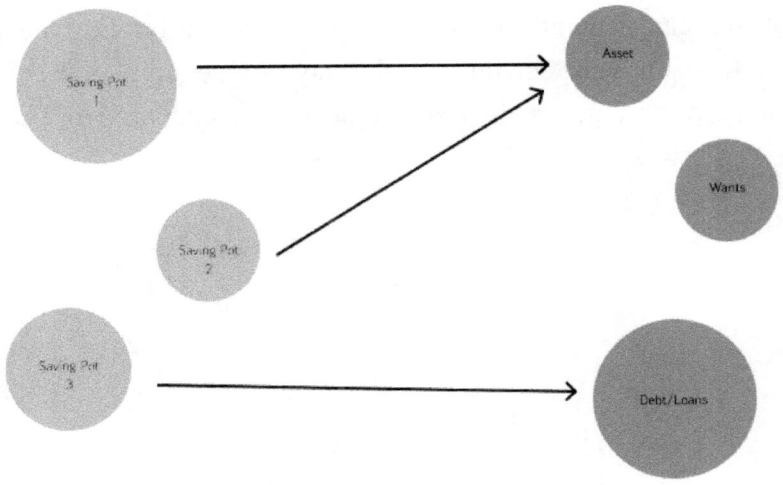

The concentrating the attack method: you use multiple saving pots for a specific goal, e.g., to purchase the asset that will generate passive income, in order to create a new saving pot.

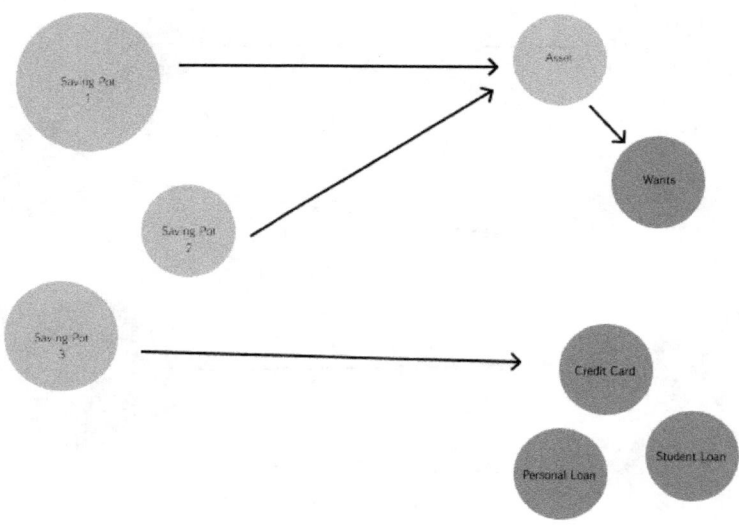

You have conquered the asset and converted it into a new saving pot that can generate passive income—more resources to expand and take on your enemies. You may divide up the debts into smaller parts, e.g., credit card, personal loan, student loan, etc.

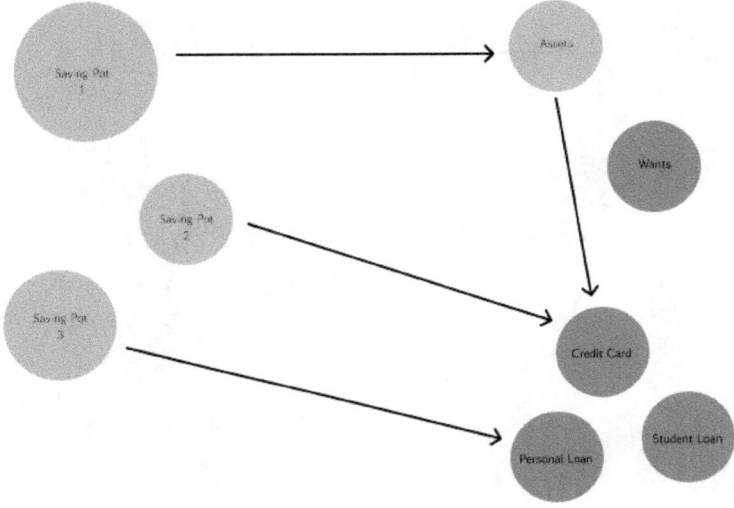

You can use the new saving pot, income generated from the asset to reduce the credit card debt until you have eliminated it. Repeat the process to target other loans/bad debt.

The strategy here is to use new passive income to reduce the debt while using your active income to create more saving pots or increasing the size of the saving pots.

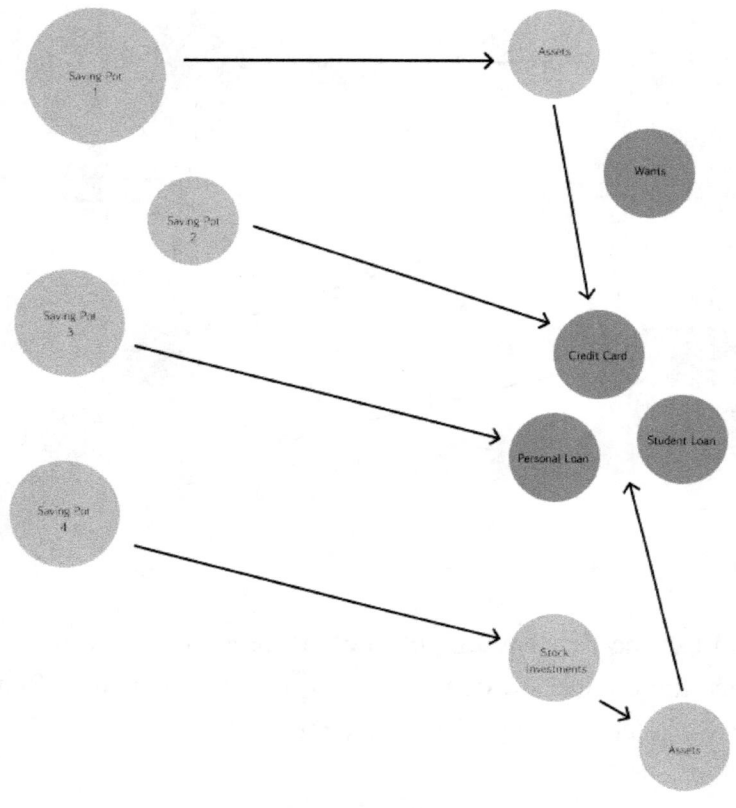

Good Debt Versus Bad Debt

Landmines, Deceptive Strongholds, and True Fortresses

On the financial battlefield, understanding the difference between good and bad debt is paramount. As we've discussed, not all debts are created equal. Some are dangerous traps, while others can be valuable allies. A good general must know his enemies and know which battle to fight, even when the enemy is in disguise.

Bad Debt: The Landmines and Deceptive Strongholds

Bad debts are like hidden landmines scattered across your financial battlefield. They are dangerous, destructive, and offer no strategic advantage whatsoever. Stepping on one of these landmines can cause significant damage to your financial health, setting you back considerably and making it much harder to reach your goals. They are like traps that will cost you time, resources, and money to recover. However, bad debt can also be disguised as something more appealing, like a seemingly valuable stronghold that turns out to be a costly mistake.

- **Credit Card Debt**

    These are the most obvious and easily identifiable landmines on the battlefield. They are easy to spot, but unfortunately, they are also incredibly easy to fall into. Credit cards offer the convenience of buying goods and services now and paying for them later. However, this convenience comes at a steep price. If you do not pay off your full balance every month, you will be charged interest.

This interest is essentially a fee for borrowing money, and it can be very high. The longer you take to pay off the debt, the more interest you will accumulate. This makes it even harder to escape the debt trap. It is like getting wounded on the battlefield; it takes time, resources, and effort to recover.

While it is best to avoid credit card debt altogether, if you are disciplined and always pay your bill in full and on time, you can actually use credit cards to your advantage. Some cards offer cash-back or reward points, which is like getting free supplies or weapons for your army. This can give you a slight edge in the battle, but only if used responsibly.

- **Payday Loans**

These are the deadliest and most destructive landmines on the battlefield, small but incredibly powerful. They are designed to be quick and easy to obtain, seemingly offering a lifeline in times of financial distress. However, they are nothing more than a cleverly disguised trap. Payday loans come with outrageously high interest rates, often trapping borrowers in a vicious cycle of debt. Each time you renew the loan, the interest and fees pile up, making it almost impossible to break free. It is like getting caught in quicksand; the more you struggle, the deeper you sink. You should never, under any circumstances, take out a payday loan. They are financial poison, and they will severely damage your chances of winning the battle.

- **Car Loans for Overpriced Vehicles**

Think of cars as vehicles to help you navigate the battlefield. They can be useful tools, but only if you choose the right one. Borrowing a large sum of money to buy a very expensive or luxurious car is like choosing a slow, heavy tank that consumes a lot of fuel when a light, agile vehicle would be more effective. The large monthly payments, along with the high costs of petrol, insurance, and maintenance, will drain your resources and severely restrict your movement on the battlefield. It is like trying to fight a battle with a weapon that is too heavy and cumbersome to wield effectively. It is much wiser to choose a car that you can comfortably afford, one that meets your transportation needs without breaking the bank. A reliable, fuel-efficient car is like a nimble, fast vehicle that allows you to manoeuvre quickly and efficiently across the battlefield, conserving your resources for more important engagements.

- **Bad Investments and Failing Businesses (The Deceptive Strongholds)**

Sometimes, bad debt disguises itself as an opportunity, a seemingly valuable stronghold that promises great returns. This could be a poorly performing investment, like stocks in a failing company or a real estate venture that loses value. Or it could be putting money into a business that is poorly managed, has a flawed business model, or is simply in a declining market. These situations are like capturing a strategic location, only to discover that it is worthless, or worse, a liability. You might have poured significant resources into acquiring what you thought was a valuable asset, only to find out that it is draining your resources and hindering your progress. This is a pyrrhic victory, a costly win that leaves you weaker than before. You have expended valuable time, effort, and resources to capture this stronghold, only to find out that it is not generating any income, or worse, it is costing you money to maintain. The resources you invested in this failed venture could have been used elsewhere, perhaps to capture a truly valuable stronghold or to eliminate dangerous landmines. This is why thorough research, due diligence, and careful planning are essential before making any investment. You need to make sure that the stronghold you are targeting is truly valuable and not a deceptive trap that will lead you to ruin. Just as a general would scout the area and gather intelligence before launching an attack, you need to investigate any potential investment thoroughly before committing your resources.

Good Debt: The Strategic Strongholds

In contrast to the destructive landmines and deceptive strongholds of bad debt, good debts are like strategic strongholds or fortified fortresses on the battlefield that are truly worth capturing. At first, they might appear to be in enemy hands, as they represent money you owe. However, if you can conquer these strongholds through careful planning and the strategic use of your saving pots, they can be transformed into valuable assets. Once under your control, these strongholds can generate income, provide strategic advantages, and significantly contribute to your overall victory in the financial battle.

- **Mortgage for a Rental Property**

    Imagine a large, imposing fortress on a hill, overlooking the entire battlefield. That is what a well-chosen rental property can be like. When you take out a mortgage to purchase a house or flat that you intend to rent out, you are essentially laying siege to a strategic location. The rent you collect from your tenants each month is like receiving tribute or taxes from the conquered territory. If you have done your calculations correctly, the monthly rental income will be higher than your mortgage payment, along with other property-related expenses such as maintenance, insurance, and property management fees. This difference is called positive cash flow, and it means you are making a profit each month. This extra income can then be used to reinforce your other saving pots, allowing you to build up your reserves, expand your territory by acquiring more properties, or even invest in other areas, further diversifying your income streams. Moreover, owning a rental property provides you with a commanding view of the surrounding area. You can monitor the property market, identify emerging trends, and make informed decisions about future investments.

- **Business Loan**

    A well-planned business loan is like securing funding to build a factory within your kingdom. This factory represents your business, and it has the potential to produce valuable goods or services that you can sell to others, generating revenue and expanding your influence. You can use the loan to purchase essential equipment, hire skilled workers, secure the necessary supplies, or cover operational costs during the initial phase of your business. The key to success is having a solid business plan, a well-defined target market, and a realistic projection of your revenue and expenses. If your business is successful, the revenue it generates will far exceed the cost of the loan repayments.

This profit then becomes a new source of income, flowing back into your "wealth accumulation" pot. This strengthens your overall financial position and provides you with the resources to reinvest in your business, further expanding its operations and increasing its profitability. The resources generated will be your supplies for your armies, and you will need to constantly replenish the supplies in order to win the battle. You can use it to improve your production line, hire more talents, or even produce a wider variety of products.

- **Strategic Stock Investments**

Certain types of stock investments can be considered good debt when approached strategically. This is like capturing a smaller, but still valuable, stronghold that generates resources for your kingdom.

- **Exchange-Traded Funds (ETFs)**
ETFs are like capturing a well-diversified fort that provides a steady stream of supplies. They are baskets of different stocks that track a particular index, like the FTSE 100. Investing in ETFs provides instant diversification,

spreading your risk across multiple companies and sectors. This is a more stable and less risky approach to stock investing, making it a good stronghold to capture for long-term growth. They are generally low-cost and offer a good way to gain exposure to the stock market without having to pick individual stocks. While they might not generate the same high returns as some individual stocks, they offer a more balanced and reliable approach to building wealth over time.

- **Blue-Chip Stocks**

Investing in blue-chip stocks is like capturing a stronghold defended by a strong and reliable garrison. Blue-chip stocks are shares of large, well-established, and financially sound companies with a long history of stable earnings and dividend payments. Companies like Unilever, Diageo, or GlaxoSmithKline are considered blue-chip companies in the UK. These companies are typically leaders in their respective industries and have a proven track record of weathering economic storms. While the prices of blue-chip stocks might not grow as rapidly as those of smaller, more volatile companies, they are generally considered safer investments. They are less likely to experience drastic price drops, and many blue-chip companies pay regular dividends to their shareholders. These dividends are like receiving regular supplies from a well-defended stronghold, providing a steady stream of income that can be reinvested or added to your other saving pots.

By strategically investing in ETFs and blue-chip stocks, you can capture strongholds that provide stability, long-term growth, and a steady stream of income in the form of dividends. These investments can be an important part of your overall financial strategy, helping you build a diversified and resilient portfolio.

How to Win the Battle

Deploying Your Saving Pots and Conquering Your Enemies

Now that you have a clear understanding of the financial battlefield, including your enemies (bad debts in the form of landmines and booby-trapped strongholds) and your potential allies (good debts in the form of true strategic strongholds), it is time to deploy your armies, your saving pots. As you will recall from earlier chapters, each saving pot represents a different division of troops, trained for a specific purpose. How you allocate these troops and how you create new troops from your income will determine your success in the game. A good general always knows how to best utilise his troops in different situations and how to raise new troops to bolster his army.

1. Divide and Conquer: Eliminating the Landmines and Booby-Trapped Strongholds

Your first and most urgent priority is to clear the battlefield of those dangerous landmines and deceptive strongholds, the bad debts. These are your primary enemies, and they must be dealt with swiftly and decisively. You must divide and conquer, attacking them from multiple angles with all the resources at your disposal. A single, all-out attack might not be effective against a well-entrenched enemy. Instead, you need a multi-pronged strategy, weakening the enemy from different sides until they are defeated.

Using Multiple Income Sources to Create New Saving Pots:

It is not just about using your existing saving pots. You can, and should, use your active income, such as your salary from your job, as well as any passive income you might have, such as rental income or dividends from investments, to create new saving pots specifically targeted at eliminating debt. Think of your active income as your main source of new recruits for your army, while your passive income is like reinforcements coming in from conquered territories.

Example: Let's say you receive a monthly salary of $3,000. Instead of treating it as one lump sum, divide it up strategically. Allocate a portion, say $500, to your existing saving pots, such as your "emergency fund" or your "house down payment" pot, that you have learnt to set up from previous chapters. Then, create a new saving pot specifically designated as your "debt elimination" pot and allocate, for example, $700 to it. This $700 is your dedicated army for attacking bad debts. You can even create multiple "debt elimination" pots, each targeting a specific debt, further dividing your forces for a more targeted attack.

Example: If you have passive income, say $200 per month from a small investment, channel that directly into your "debt elimination" pot(s). Now your debt-fighting army has $900 per month to deploy. The more sources of income you have, the more troops you can recruit to fight your debt battles.

Attacking Debt from Multiple Angles with Numerical Examples:

Once you have your "debt elimination" pot, or multiple pots dedicated to debt repayment, you can start attacking your debts from different angles, just like a general laying siege to a fortress from all sides. This "divide and conquer" strategy weakens the debt's hold on you and accelerates your path to freedom.

Let's say you have the following debts:

- Credit Card 1: $1,000 balance, 18% APR
- Credit Card 2: $500 balance, 20% APR
- Personal Loan: $2,000 balance, 10% APR

Scenario 1: Linear Attack (Traditional Approach)

You decide to focus on paying off Credit Card 2 first using only extra payment on top of the minimum payment because it has the highest interest rate (Avalanche Method). You allocate $200 per month to debt repayment, making only the minimum payments on Credit Card 1 and the personal loan.

- **Month 1:** You pay off a significant portion of Credit Card 2, reducing the balance to around $300 (assuming a minimum payment of around $25). However, interest accrues on all three debts, adding to their balances. Credit card 1 will have around $15 interest, and the personal loan will have around $16.67 interest.

- **Month 3:** You might have paid off Credit Card 2. But interest has continued to accrue on Credit Card 1 (around $45 total) and the loan (around $50 total).

- **Month 6:** You are now focusing on Credit Card 1, with a balance of around $880. Progress is slow due to only making the minimum payment and accumulated interest for the first 3 months.

- **Month 12:** You might have made a dent in Credit Card 1, reducing it to around $400, and started on the personal loan, with a balance of around $1700. It will take another 9 months to fully pay off all the debt.

In this scenario, even with extra payment on top of the minimum payment, it would take you **21 months to** pay off all debts. Total payment would be around **$3900.**

Scenario 2: Multi-Angled Attack (Divide and Conquer)

You have your $900 "debt elimination" pot. You decide to divide it as follows:

- Credit Card 1: $300
- Credit Card 2: $200
- Personal Loan: $400

- **Month 1:** You significantly reduce the balance on all three debts. Credit card 1 balance is $715, credit card 2 is $316, and personal loan is $1616.

- **Month 3:** Credit card 2 is paid off. You reallocate that $200 to the other two debts. Now you're paying $450 to Credit Card 1 and $450 to the personal loan. Credit card 1 balance is around $176, and the personal loan is around $900.

- **Month 4:** Credit card 1 is paid off. You now have the full $900 to focus on the personal loan.

- **Month 6:** The personal loan is paid off.

Result: By dividing your debt elimination pot and attacking from multiple angles, you've paid off all your debts in **6 months**! You've also saved a significant amount on interest payments; the total payment is around **$3500**. The multi-angled approach is clearly much faster and more cost-effective.

Dealing with Bad Investments

For bad investments that are losing money, the strategy is different. You need to **cut** your losses. This is like abandoning a captured fortress that turns out to be a booby-trapped stronghold, a liability disguised as an asset, rigged to explode and drain your resources. It is better to retreat and redeploy your resources elsewhere than to keep pouring money into a losing venture.

- **Sell the poorly performing assets:** Even if it means taking a loss, sell the investments that are consistently losing money. Holding onto them in the hope that they will recover is often a mistake. This is like abandoning a faulty stronghold that is draining your resources.

- **Redeploy the recovered funds:** Use the proceeds from selling these assets to pay down other debts, particularly those with high interest rates. Alternatively, you can reinvest the money in more promising opportunities after thorough research and due diligence. This is like using the salvaged resources from a failed venture to strengthen your other positions on the battlefield.

- **Learn from your mistakes:** Do not let pride or the hope of recouping your losses cloud your judgment. A good general learns from every battle, even the ones they lose. Analyse why the investment failed and use that knowledge to make better decisions in the future.

By creating new saving pots from your active and passive income and attacking your debts from multiple angles, you are effectively dividing and conquering your enemies, eliminating them much faster than you would by using a single approach. You are weakening their hold on you, freeing up your resources, and gaining momentum towards victory.

Building Your Empire: Acquiring Strategic Strongholds

Once you have cleared the battlefield of bad debts, or significantly reduced them, you can start thinking about strategically acquiring good debts, those true fortresses that can generate income and help you expand your empire. This is where your specialised saving pots, along with your active and passive income, come into play. Remember, each saving pot, as you learnt in earlier chapters, is like a division of your army, trained for a specific purpose, and your income provides the resources to train and equip new divisions. You are no longer just defending your initial territory; you are now going on the offensive, expanding your kingdom, and securing valuable resources.

- **Using Existing Saving Pots:** Your existing saving pots, such as your "house down payment" pot or your "business start-up" pot, can be used to make a down payment on a rental property or secure a business loan, respectively. These are like using your well-trained troops to lay siege to a valuable fortress. You have been preparing for this, and now you are ready to deploy your forces.

- **Creating New Saving Pots for Specific Strongholds:** You can also create new saving pots specifically for acquiring certain strongholds. For example, if you want to invest in a particular stock or ETF, you can start a new savings pot dedicated to that purpose. This is like training a new division of troops specifically for a particular type of battle or for capturing a specific type of fortress. You are tailoring your forces to the specific challenges and opportunities of each stronghold.

- **Leveraging Active and Passive Income:** Your active income (like your salary) and any passive income you generate (like rental income or dividends) should be continuously channelled into your saving pots, both existing and new. This is like constantly recruiting and training new troops to reinforce your army and expand your capacity to capture more strongholds. Every dollar you earn should be strategically allocated, with a portion going towards building your empire. Think of your income as the lifeblood of your kingdom, constantly replenishing your resources and fuelling your expansion. You are not just spending your money; you are investing it in building a stronger and more prosperous future.

The Virtuous Cycle: Turning Strongholds into Saving Pots and Expanding Your Forces

This is where your strategic brilliance really shines. The true power of this strategy lies in your ability to turn those conquered strongholds (good debts) into new sources of income, effectively creating new saving pots and expanding your empire. This creates a virtuous cycle, a positive feedback loop where your assets generate income, which is then used to acquire more assets, generating even more income, and so on. Your kingdom will grow stronger and more prosperous with each turn of this cycle. It is like a snowball effect, but instead of eliminating debt, you are accumulating wealth, building a powerful and self-sustaining financial empire.

Example: Rental Property

- You use your "house down payment" pot of $20,000 and take out a mortgage to buy a rental property for $100,000.
- You rent out the property for $800 per month.
- Your mortgage payment is $400 per month, and other expenses (insurance, maintenance) are $100 per month.

- **Positive Cash Flow:** $800 (rent) - $400 (mortgage) - $100 (expenses) = $300 per month.
- You create a new saving pot called "rental income" and channel the $300 into it each month.
- **After 1 year:** Your "rental income" pot has $3,600.
- **After 5 years:** Your "rental income" pot has $18,000. You now have enough for a down payment on another rental property, or you can add it to another savings pot to diversify your investments.
- **After 10 years:** Your "rental income" pot has $36,000. If you bought another rental property in year 5, your total rental income pot would be significantly larger, around $72,000, not counting the potential appreciation of the property value or the increase in rent.

Example: Business Loan

- You secure a business loan of $10,000 to start a small online business.
- You use the loan to build a website, purchase inventory, and market your products.
- In the first year, your business generates $20,000 in revenue.
- Your expenses, including loan repayments, are $15,000.
- **Profit:** $20,000 (revenue) - $15,000 (expenses) = $5,000.
- You channel this $5,000 profit into your "wealth accumulation" pot.
- In the second year, your business grows, generating $30,000 in revenue.
- Your expenses are now $20,000 due to expansion.
- **Profit:** $30,000 - $20,000 = $10,000

- Your "wealth accumulation" pot grows by another $10,000. You can now reinvest this money to further expand your business, increasing your profit even more in subsequent years.
- **After 5 years:** If you have reinvested your profits wisely, your business might be generating significantly more revenue. Your "wealth accumulation" pot could be substantial, allowing you to make further investments or diversify into other income streams.

Example: Stock Investments (ETFs and Blue-Chip Stocks)

- You invest $1,000 in a blue-chip stock that pays a 4% annual dividend.
- **Year 1:** You receive $40 in dividends. You reinvest this into your "stock investment" pot.
- **Year 5:** Assuming the stock price and dividend remain stable, you'll have earned around $200 in dividends (this will be higher if you have purchased more stock), which you've reinvested. Your initial $1,000 investment might have also grown in value, let's say to $1,200.
- You also invest $50 per month into an ETF.
- **Year 1:** You've invested $600. Assuming a modest 5% annual return, your investment is now worth around $630.
- **Year 5:** You've invested $3,000. With compounding returns, your investment could be worth over $3,800.
- **Year 10:** You've invested $6,000. With compounding returns, your investment could be worth over $9,000.

These examples demonstrate how your saving pots can grow exponentially over time through the virtuous cycle. The income generated by your assets is reinvested, creating more income, and so on. This is how you build real wealth and achieve your financial goals. The amount in the saving pot will increase exponentially as you keep reinvesting the profit you earned from your investment.

By diligently following these steps, creating new saving pots from your active and passive income, deploying your resources strategically to eliminate bad debt, acquiring good debt, and reinvesting the income generated by your assets, you will be well on your way to winning the financial battle, conquering your enemies, expanding your empire, and achieving your goal of building a million-dollar kingdom.

You have learnt how to deploy your saving pots effectively, eliminate bad debts, and acquire good debts that generate income. You are well on your way to building a powerful financial kingdom. However, just like any kingdom, your financial empire needs protection from unforeseen threats and requires a strong, strategic leader to guide it to long-term prosperity. This is where creating a strong financial defence, constant monitoring, adaptability, and cultivating a winning mindset become crucial.

Building a Strong Financial Defence

A well-defended kingdom is not easily conquered. You need to build a strong financial defence to protect your hard-earned wealth from unexpected events and economic downturns.

- **Emergency Fund (Your Fortress Walls):** As covered in previous chapters, your emergency fund is your first line of defence. It is like the strong walls surrounding your kingdom, protecting you from sudden attacks like job loss, medical emergencies, or unexpected home repairs. Aim to have at least three to six months' worth of essential living expenses in an easily accessible savings pot. This will provide a safety net, allowing you to weather any financial storms without having to sell off your assets or go into debt. Regularly replenish this fund, treating it as a non-negotiable part of your budget.

- **Insurance (Your Shield):** Insurance is like a shield that protects you from specific risks. Different types of insurance protect different aspects of your kingdom. Health insurance safeguards you from crippling medical bills. Car insurance protects you from the financial burden of accidents. Home insurance protects your property from damage or theft. Life insurance provides a safety net for your loved ones in case of your untimely demise. Having the right insurance coverage is essential to prevent unforeseen events from derailing your financial plans. Do your research, compare policies, and choose coverage that best suits your needs and budget.

- **Diversification (Your Diversified Army):** Just as a wise general diversifies his troops, you should diversify your investments. Do not put all your eggs in one basket. Spread your investments across different asset classes, such as stocks, bonds, real estate, and perhaps even a small allocation to alternative investments. This reduces your risk because if one investment performs poorly, others might perform well, balancing out your overall returns. Diversification is like having different divisions in your army, each with its own strengths and weaknesses, prepared for different types of battles. This way your kingdom will not be easily defeated if one division suffers losses.

Constant Monitoring and Adaptability

The financial battlefield is constantly changing. Economic conditions shift, markets fluctuate, and new opportunities and threats emerge. As the ruler of your financial kingdom, you must remain vigilant and adapt to these changes.

- **Regular Reviews (Surveying the Battlefield):** Regularly review your financial situation. Monitor your investments, track your spending, and reassess your debts. This is like surveying the battlefield to assess your position, identify potential threats, and spot new opportunities. Schedule these reviews at least quarterly or semiannually. This is when you would make a battle plan, making sure that your troops are deployed in the right places.

- **Budgeting (Your Supply Lines):** Your budget is your financial roadmap, and it needs to be regularly reviewed and adjusted. Track your income and expenses, identify areas where you can save money, and make sure your spending aligns with your financial goals. This is like managing your supply lines, ensuring that your troops have the resources they need to fight effectively. There are many tools available to help with budgeting, such as spreadsheets, budgeting software, and mobile apps. Find a method that works for you and stick to it.

- **Adaptability (Strategic Retreat and Redeployment):** Be prepared to change your strategy if necessary. If an investment is consistently underperforming, do not be afraid to sell it and redeploy the funds elsewhere. If your income or expenses change, adjust your budget accordingly. This is like a general adapting to changing circumstances on the battlefield, retreating from a losing position, or redeploying troops to where they are needed most. Do not be afraid to change your battle plan if your existing plan is not working out.

Cultivating the Mindset of a Winner

"Always take the winning move, for it will guarantee your win."

Building and protecting a financial empire requires more than just strategic planning and tactical execution. It requires the mindset of a winner, a belief in your ability to achieve your goals, and a commitment to continuous learning and improvement.

- **Patience (The Long Game):** Building wealth takes time. It is a marathon, not a sprint. There will be ups and downs, periods of rapid growth and periods of slow progress. Do not be discouraged by short-term setbacks. Stay focused on your long-term goals and trust in the process. Remember that every step you take, no matter how small, is bringing you closer to your destination. Just like in a chess game, the saving pots need time to build up your armies and slowly conquer your enemies and the strategic points.

- **Discipline (Following the Plan):** Sticking to your financial plan, even when faced with temptations or distractions, is crucial. Avoid impulsive spending, resist the urge to chase quick returns, and stay committed to your long-term strategy. This is like a general maintaining discipline within their ranks, ensuring that every soldier follows the battle plan. Make sure that you have full control of your troops and deploy them to where they are needed.

- **Continuous Learning (Sharpening Your Sword):** The financial world is complex and constantly evolving. To succeed, you must commit to continuous learning. Read books, articles, and websites about personal finance and investing. Attend seminars or workshops. Seek out mentors or advisors who can provide guidance and support. The more you know, the better equipped you will be to make informed decisions and adapt to changing circumstances. This is like a general constantly studying new tactics, learning about new weapons, and improving their understanding of warfare. You need to constantly improve your knowledge about finance in order to win the battle.

- **Goal Setting (Your Guiding Star):** Clearly defined financial goals are essential for success. They provide direction, motivation, and a sense of purpose. Set SMART goals—Specific, Measurable, Achievable, Relevant, and Time-bound. For example, instead of saying, "I want to save more money," set a goal like, "I want to save $10,000 for a down payment on a house in the next two years." Regularly review your goals and adjust them as needed.

This is like a general setting clear objectives for their troops, providing a clear path to victory.

- **Positive Visualisation (Envisioning Victory):** Take some time each day to visualise yourself achieving your financial goals. Imagine what your life will be like when you have reached your first million, when you are financially free. This positive visualisation can help to strengthen your belief in your ability to succeed and keep you motivated during challenging times. This is like a general inspiring his troops with a vision of a better future, fuelling their determination to fight for victory.

Sample Simulation

Let's continue with the example from the previous chapter.

Starting Point (Year 3):

- Total Savings (in one general saving pot): $41,014.75
- Emergency Fund: $0
- Stock Investment Pot: $0
- House Down Payment Pot: $0
- Rental Income Pot: $0
- Job: Lead Web Developer - $3,500 per month (after tax).
- Freelance Graphic Design: $1,000 per month.
- Photography: $500 per month.
- Total Monthly Income: $5,000

Phase 3: Capturing a Major Stronghold and Building Defences (Year 4-5)

Actions taken:

1. Property Purchase: You use $40,000 from your general saving pot as a down payment for a $200,000 rental property, taking out a mortgage for the remaining $160,000. This is a major stronghold captured.

    ◦ Debt Acquired: $160,000 (Mortgage 1) at 4% interest rate, 30-year term. Monthly payment: Approximately $764.

2. Rental Income: You rent out the property for $1,500 per month.

    ◦ Positive Cash Flow: $1,500 (rent) - $764 (mortgage) - $300 (expenses) = $436 per month.

3. New Saving Pots: You create new saving pots:

    ◦ Emergency Fund: Recognising the need for a safety net, you start rebuilding your emergency fund, allocating $1,000 per month to it.
    ◦ Rental Income Pot: You channel the $436 positive cash flow into it each month. You also allocate $600 from your salary to this pot, totalling $1,000 per month.
    ◦ Stock Investment Pot: You start to learn about stock investment, allocating $500 per month to this pot.

4. Remaining Allocation: After allocating to the new saving pots, you have $2,000 left for your essential living expenses.

5. Annual Salary Increase: Your salary increases by 3% annually.

6. Year 5 Promotion and Bonus: You receive a promotion to Senior Web Developer, increasing your salary by an additional 10% from Year 5 onwards. You also receive a one-time performance bonus of $5,000 in Year 5, which you add to your General Savings Pot.

Outcome after Year 4-5:

	Year 3	Year 4	Year 5	Change (Year 4-5)
Salary (Monthly)	$3,500	$3,605	$4,066	+$566 (+16.17%)
Emergency Fund	$0	$12,000	$24,000	+$24,000 (+100%)
Stock Investment Pot	$0	$6,210	$13,000	+$13,000 (+100%)
Rental Income Pot	$0	$12,000	$24,000	+$24,000 (+100%)
General Savings Pot	$41,014.75	$1,014.75	$6,014.75	-$35,000 (-85.34%)
Rental Property Value	$0	$204,000	$208,080	+$8,080 (+4%)
Equity in Rental Property	$0	$3,357	$10,000	+$10,000 (+100%)
Total Assets	$41,014.75	$238,581.75	$285,094.75	+$244,080 (+595.08%)
Mortgage 1	$0	$156,643	$153,106	-$6,894 (-4.3%)
Total Liabilities	$0	$156,643	$153,106	-$6,894 (-4.3%)
Net Worth	$41,014.75	$81,938.75	$131,988.75	+$90,974 (+221.81%)

Key summary:

- Your salary has increased by 3% in Year 4 and an additional 10% in Year 5 due to a promotion, plus you received a bonus.
- Your net worth is now $131,988.75.
- You now own a rental property valued at $208,080 (assuming 2% annual appreciation), which is a significant asset.
- Your Emergency Fund is being built up for protection.
- You're starting to invest in stocks, with your Stock Investment Pot showing modest growth.
- Your Rental Income Pot is growing well, thanks to the positive cash flow from your rental property.
- Your Equity in the rental property is increasing as you pay down the mortgage.
- Mortgage 1 decreased by $6,894 in 2 years.

Phase 4: Expanding the Empire and Hitting a Landmine (Year 6-8)

Objective: Acquire a second rental property, continue stock investments, and recover from a setback.

Actions taken:

1. Second Rental Property: You use your accumulated Rental Income Pot ($24,000) plus $16,000 from your General Savings Pot for another $200,000 rental property. You obtain a mortgage for the remaining $160,000.

- Debt Acquired: $160,000 (Mortgage 2) at 4.5% interest rate, 30-year term. Monthly payment: Approximately $811.

2. Rental Income: You rent out the second property for $1,400 per month.

    - Positive Cash Flow: $1,400 (rent) - $811 (mortgage) - $300 (expenses) = $289 per month. This brings your total rental income to $689 per month.

3. Landmine! Your freelance graphic design work unexpectedly dries up, losing you $1,000 per month in income.

4. Adapting to the Landmine:

    - You temporarily reduce your Stock Investment Pot contributions to $200 per month.
    - You continue to contribute to your Emergency Fund, but reduces it to $800 per month.
    - You now allocate $1,000 to your rental income pot.
    - You now allocate $1,000 to your general saving pot.

5. Using Investment Income to Pay Down Mortgage: You use the dividends generated from your Stock Investment Pot (assume around $60 per month) to make extra payments on your first rental property mortgage.

6. Annual Salary Increase: Your salary increases by 3% annually.

Outcome after Year 6-8:

	Year 6	Year 7	Year 8	Change (Year 6-8)
Salary (Monthly)	$4,188	$4,314	$4,443	+$377 (+9.27%)
Emergency Fund	$33,600	$43,200	$52,800	+$28,800 (+120%)
Stock Investment Pot	$15,780	$19,007	$22,735	+$9,735 (+74.88%)
Rental Income Pot	$36,000	$48,000	$60,000	+$36,000 (+150%)
General Savings Pot	$18,014.75	$30,014.75	$42,014.75	+$36,000 (+598.54%)
Rental Property Value 1	$212,242	$216,486	$220,816	+$12,736 (+6.12%)
Equity in Rental Property 1	$16,114	$22,679	$29,735	+$19,735 (+197.35%)
Rental Property Value 2	$204,000	$208,080	$212,242	+$212,242 (+100%)
Equity in Rental Property 2	$3,235	$6,615	$10,147	+$10,147 (+100%)
Total Assets	$338,985.75	$394,001.75	$450,492.75	+$165,398 (+57.99%)

Mortgage 1	$149,517	$145,728	$141,726	-$11,380 (-7.43%)
Mortgage 2	$156,765	$153,371	$149,806	-$10,194 (-6.37%)
Total Liabilities	$306,282	$299,099	$291,532	+$138,426 (+90.41%)
Net Worth	$32,703.75	$94,902.75	$158,960.75	+$26,972 (+20.44%)

Key summary:

- Your assets have grown significantly to $450,492.75. You've captured a second rental property, and your saving pots are growing.
- Your liabilities have also increased due to the second mortgage.
- Your net worth is now at $159,050.75.
- You successfully navigated a "landmine" (loss of freelance income) by adjusting your savings strategy.
- You are using a small amount of your stock dividends to pay down your mortgage faster.
- Rental property value has been appreciating at 2% per year.
- Your salary is increasing by 3% each year.

Phase 5: Recovering, Rebuilding, and Hitting a Booby Trap (Year 9-12)

Objective: Recover from the landmine, rebuild investment momentum, and deal with a bad investment.

Actions taken:

1. New Income Source: You find a part-time teaching position in web development, earning $800 per month. You add this to your general saving pot.

2. Increased Stock Investment: With your increased income, you gradually raise your Stock Investment Pot contributions back to $500 per month.

3. Booby-Trapped Stronghold: You invest $5,000 from your Rental Income Pot into what you believe is a promising tech start-up (a seemingly attractive stronghold). Unfortunately, the start-up fails, and you lose your entire investment.

4. Continued Savings: You continue to contribute $800 to your emergency fund, $1,689 to your rental income pot and $1,300 to your general saving pot.

5. Using Rental Income to Pay Down Mortgage: You now use $300 per month from your Rental Income Pot to make extra payments on your second rental property mortgage, further accelerating debt reduction. You continue to use $300 per month from your Rental Income Pot to make extra payments on your first rental property mortgage.

6. Using Investment Income to Pay Down Mortgage: You use the dividends generated from your Stock Investment Pot (assume around $150 per month) to make extra payments on your first rental property mortgage.

7. **Annual Salary Increase:** Your salary increases by 3% annually.

Outcome after Year 9-12:

	Year 9	Year 10	Year 11	Year 12	Change (Year 9-12)
Salary (Monthly)	$4,576	$4,714	$4,855	$5,001	+$558 (+12.56%)
Emergency Fund	$62,400	$72,000	$81,600	$91,200	+$38,400 (+72.73%)
Stock Investment Pot	$29,627	$37,435	$46,246	$56,156	+$33,421 (+146.97%)
Rental Income Pot	$80,268	$99,879	$118,798	$136,989	+$76,989 (+128.32%)
General Savings Pot	$57,614.75	$73,214.75	$88,814.75	$104,414.75	+$62,400 (+148.52%)
Rental Property Value 1	$225,232	$229,737	$234,332	$239,018	+$18,202 (+8.24%)
Equity in Rental Property 1	$37,398	$45,642	$54,507	$64,035	+$34,300 (+115.35%)
Rental Property Value 2	$216,486	$220,816	$225,232	$229,737	+$17,495 (+8.24%)
Equity in Rental Property 2	$13,968	$18,079	$22,498	$27,249	+$17,102 (+168.54%)
Total Assets	$523,293.75	$596,801.75	$672,027.75	$748,798.75	+$298,216 (+66.19%)
Mortgage 1	$137,516	$133,059	$128,337	$123,328	-$18,398 (-12.98%)
Mortgage 2	$145,976	$141,911	$137,600	$133,022	-$16,784 (-11.2%)
Total Liabilities	$283,492	$274,970	$265,937	$256,350	-$35,182 (-12.07%)

| Net Worth | $239,801.75 | $321,831.75 | $406,090.75 | $492,448.75 | +$333,398 (+209.62%) |

Key summary:

- You successfully recovered from the "booby trap" (bad investment) thanks to your diversified income and saving pots.
- Your net worth is growing steadily and now stands at $492,448.75.
- You are aggressively paying down your mortgages using rental income and stock dividends.
- Your Emergency Fund is very well funded.
- Rental properties value have been appreciating at 2% per year.
- Your salary is increasing by 3% each year.

Phase 6: Building a Merchandise Business and The Million-Dollar Kingdom (Year 13-20)

Objective: Launch a merchandise business, reach $1 million and continue growing the empire.

Actions taken:

1. Merchandise Business: Leveraging your graphic design skills, you start a small online merchandise business selling branded apparel and accessories related to web development. You invest $5,000 from your general saving

pot to get it started. The business generates an average profit of $1,500 per month after expenses. You channel this profit into a new saving pot - "Merchandise Business Pot".

2. Continued Investment and Reinvestment: You continue to invest in stocks, reinvest rental income, and maintain your emergency fund contributions. You increase your monthly stock investment to $1,000 per month, rental income pot contribution to $2,589 per month, general saving to $1,000 per month.

3. Rental Income Growth: With consistent rental income and reinvestment, your Rental Income Pot grows significantly. You continue using a portion of it for extra mortgage payments.

4. Increased Stock Dividends: As your Stock Investment Pot grows, it generates more substantial dividends (around $300 per month), which you also use to make extra mortgage payments.

5. Annual Salary Increase: Your salary increases by 3% annually.

Outcome after Year 13-20:

	Year 13	Year 14	Year 15	Year 16
Salary (Monthly)	$5,151	$5,306	$5,465	$5,629
Emergency Fund	$100,800	$110,400	$120,000	$129,600
Stock Investment Pot	$70,465	$86,834	$105,556	$126,956
Rental Income Pot	$170,757	$207,768	$248,358	$292,911
General Savings Pot	$111,414.75	$123,414.75	$135,414.75	$147,414.75
Merchandise Business Pot	$18,000	$36,000	$54,000	$72,000
Rental Property Value 1	$243,798	$248,674	$253,648	$258,721
Equity in Rental Property 1	$74,323	$85,380	$97,103	$109,706
Rental Property Value 2	$234,332	$239,018	$243,798	$248,674
Equity in Rental Property 2	$33,272	$39,750	$46,714	$54,199
Total Assets	$882,261.75	$1,022,438.75	$1,175,223.75	$1,346,329.75
Mortgage 1	$117,998	$112,367	$106,410	$100,100
Mortgage 2	$128,988	$124,666	$120,032	$115,058
Total Liabilities	$246,986	$237,033	$226,442	$215,158
Net Worth	$635,275.75	$785,405.75	$948,781.75	$1,131,171.75

	Year 17	Year 18	Year 19	Year 20	Change (Year 13-20)
Salary (Monthly)	$5,797	$5,971	$6,150	$6,335	+$1,334 (+26.67%)
Emergency Fund	$139,200	$148,800	$158,400	$168,000	+$76,800 (+84.21%)
Stock Investment Pot	$151,390	$179,250	$210,976	$247,044	+$190,888 (+339.93%)
Rental Income Pot	$341,851	$441,607	$500,684	$571,633	+$434,644 (+317.36%)
General Savings Pot	$159,414.75	$171,414.75	$183,414.75	$195,414.75	+$96,000 (+96.57%)
Merchandise Business Pot	$90,000	$108,000	$126,000	$144,000	+$144,000 (+100%)
Rental Property Value 1	$263,895	$269,173	$274,557	$280,048	+$41,030 (+17.17%)
Equity in Rental Property 1	$112,727	$115,748	$118,769	$121,790	+$57,755 (+90.19%)
Rental Property Value 2	$253,648	$258,721	$263,895	$269,173	+$39,436 (+17.17%)
Equity in Rental Property 2	$62,242	$70,882	$79,522	$88,162	+$60,913 (+223.54%)
Total Assets	$1,471,099.75	$1,634,863.75	$1,817,051.75	$2,039,755.75	+$1,291,057 (+172.45%)
Mortgage 1	$93,407	$86,298	$78,742	$70,708	-$52,620 (-42.67%)
Mortgage 2	$109,715	$103,973	$97,803	$91,173	-$41,849 (-31.46%)
Total Liabilities	$203,122	$190,271	$176,545	$161,881	-$94,469 (-36.85%)

| Net Worth | $1,267,977.75 | $1,444,592.75 | $1,640,506.75 | $1,877,874.75 | +$1,385,526 (+281.41%) |

Key summary:

- Your merchandise business is a success, generating a healthy profit and adding a significant income stream.
- You are aggressively paying down your mortgages with rental income and stock dividends, significantly reducing your liabilities.
- Your net worth has surpassed $1 million and is growing rapidly due to your diversified income streams, strategic investments, and debt reduction.
- Rental property value has been appreciating at 2% per year.
- Your salary is increasing by 3% each year.

Phase 7: The Debt Free and The Million-Dollar Kingdom (Year 21-22)

Objective: Pay off all the debt, reach $1 million and continue growing the empire.

Actions taken:

1. Pay off all the debt: Now you have enough money in your rental income pot to pay off both mortgages. You pay off $161,881 worth of debt. Now you have no debt.

2. Continued Investment and Reinvestment: You continue to invest in stocks, reinvests rental income, and maintains her

emergency fund contributions. You allocate $4,500 per month to rental income pot contribution since no more mortgage payments, general saving to $500 per month. You are also allocating $1,000 per month to your Merchandise Business Pot, and $1,500 per month to your stock investment pot.

3. Rental Income Growth: With consistent rental income and reinvestment, your Rental Income Pot grows significantly.

4. Increased Stock Dividends: As your Stock Investment Pot grows, it generates more substantial dividends (around $800 per month), which you also use to invest in the stock investment pot.

Outcome after Year 21-22:

	Year 20	Year 21	Year 22	Change (Year 21-22)
Salary (Monthly)	$6,335	$6,525	$6,721	+$386 (+6.09%)
Emergency Fund	$168,000	$177,600	$187,200	+$19,200 (+11.43%)
Stock Investment Pot	$247,044	$334,225	$442,592	+$195,548 (+79.16%)
Rental Income Pot	$571,633	$625,633	$679,633	+$108,000 (+18.89%)
General Savings Pot	$195,414.75	$201,414.75	$207,414.75	+$12,000 (+6.14%)
Merchandise Business Pot	$144,000	$156,000	$168,000	+$24,000 (+16.67%)
Rental Property Value 1	$280,048	$285,649	$291,362	+$11,314 (+4.04%)

Equity in Rental Property 1	$176,283	$176,283	$176,283	$0
Rental Property Value 2	$269,173	$274,556	$280,047	+$10,874 (+4.04%)
Equity in Rental Property 2	$88,162	$88,162	$88,162	$0
Total Assets	$2,039,755.75	$2,219,522.75	$2,420,693.75	+$380,938 (+18.68%)
Mortgage 1	$70,708	$0	$0	-$70,708 (-100%)
Mortgage 2	$91,173	$0	$0	-$91,173 (-100%)
Total Liabilities	$161,881	$0	$0	-$161,881 (-100%)
Net Worth	$1,877,874.75	$2,219,522.75		

Disclaimer:

This example is a simplified illustration of a potential journey to building a million-dollar net worth. It is intended for educational purposes only and should not be considered financial advice. The figures used for income, expenses, investment returns, property appreciation, and other variables are illustrative and based on certain assumptions. They do not represent guaranteed outcomes and may not reflect real-world conditions.

In a real-life scenario, it's important to consider the following:

- **Pension Contributions:** This example does not include contributions to a workplace pension scheme or other retirement accounts, which can significantly impact long-term wealth accumulation.

- **Salary Increases and Bonuses:** While the example factored in some salary increases, a promotion and a bonus, the actual trajectory of your career and income may vary.

- **Investment Returns:** The example assumes a consistent 7% average annual return on stock investments. Actual stock market returns can fluctuate significantly from year to year, and there is always a risk of loss.

- **Property Appreciation:** The example assumes a 2% annual appreciation in property values. Actual property appreciation rates can vary depending on location, market conditions, and other factors.

- **Interest Rates:** Mortgage interest rates can change over time, affecting monthly payments and the overall cost of borrowing.

- **Taxes:** The example does not account for various taxes, such as income tax, capital gains tax, and property taxes, which can impact your overall financial situation.

- **Inflation:** The example does not factor in the effects of inflation, which can erode the purchasing power of money over time.

- **Unexpected Events:** Life is unpredictable, and unexpected events (e.g., job loss, medical emergencies, economic downturns) can significantly impact your financial journey.

- **Personal Circumstances:** This example is based on a hypothetical individual's circumstances. Your own financial journey will be unique and depend on your individual income, expenses, risk tolerance, and financial goals.

It is crucial to conduct thorough research, seek professional financial advice tailored to your individual circumstances, and carefully consider the risks involved before making any financial decisions.

This example should serve as a starting point for your own financial planning, not as a definitive roadmap. Remember that your own path to financial success will likely involve its own unique set of challenges and opportunities. The key is to stay informed, adaptable, and committed to your long-term goals.

Beyond the First Million

Reaching the million-dollar milestone is a significant achievement, a testament to your strategic planning, disciplined execution, and resilience in the face of challenges. However, it marks not the end of your financial journey, but rather a transition into a new phase – one of maintaining and growing your wealth. Now that you have built your empire, your focus shifts to preservation, continued expansion, and securing your financial legacy for the future.

Protecting Your Assets

Now that you have accumulated substantial wealth, protecting it becomes paramount. You have built your kingdom, and you would need to defend it at all costs. Complacency at this stage can be detrimental.

- **Regular Portfolio Reviews:** Continue to monitor your investments diligently. Just as a ruler must regularly inspect their kingdom, you must review your portfolio's performance at least annually, if not more frequently. Rebalance your portfolio as needed to maintain your desired asset allocation and risk profile. Market fluctuations can shift your asset allocation over time. Rebalancing involves selling some of your assets that have performed well and buying more of those that have underperformed to bring your portfolio back in line with your original plan. This helps to manage risk and ensure that you are not overly exposed to any one asset class.

- **Insurance Review:** Periodically review your insurance coverage to ensure it adequately protects your assets and income. As your wealth grows, your insurance needs may change. Consider increasing your liability coverage, adding an umbrella policy for extra protection, and reviewing your property insurance to ensure it reflects the current value of your assets.

- **Estate Planning:** Engage an estate planning professional to create or update your will, trust, and other relevant documents. This ensures that your assets are distributed according to your wishes after your death, minimising potential disputes and ensuring a smooth transition for your beneficiaries. A well-structured estate plan can also help to minimise estate taxes, preserving more of your wealth for future generations. This is similar to planning the line of succession for your kingdom.

- **Asset Protection Strategies:** Depending on your circumstances and the nature of your assets, consider implementing asset protection strategies. This might involve setting up trusts, limited liability companies (LLCs), or other legal structures to shield your assets from potential creditors or lawsuits. This is particularly important if you own a business or have significant real estate holdings. Seek advice from a qualified legal professional to determine the best strategies for your situation.

Continued Wealth Growth

Reaching the million-dollar mark should not be the end of your investment journey. You would still need to conquer more land to expand your kingdom further. Continued growth is essential to outpace inflation, fund your future needs, and build a lasting legacy.

- **Reinvesting Income:** Continue to reinvest the income generated from your assets (rental income, dividends, business profits). This allows the power of compounding to continue working its magic, further accelerating your wealth growth. You can reinvest this income back into your existing investments, or you can use it to explore new investment opportunities. The virtuous cycle that helped you reach your first million will continue to be your ally in this phase.

- **Diversification:** Maintain a well-diversified portfolio across different asset classes, such as stocks, bonds, real estate, and potentially alternative investments. Diversification helps to reduce risk and improve long-term returns. As your wealth grows, you might consider diversifying into new asset classes that were not previously accessible, such as private equity or venture capital.

- **Tax Optimisation:** Implement tax-efficient investment strategies to minimise your tax liability and maximise your after-tax returns. Consult with a tax advisor to explore strategies such as using tax-advantaged accounts, tax-loss harvesting, and making charitable donations. You want to minimise the taxes taken by other kingdoms.

- **Exploring New Opportunities:** Remain open to new investment opportunities that may arise. As your wealth and experience grow, you may be able to access investments that were previously unavailable to you. This could include investing in private businesses, real estate development projects, or other alternative assets. However, always conduct thorough due diligence and seek professional advice before making any significant investment decisions.

Lifestyle and Spending

Reaching the million-dollar mark may tempt you to significantly increase your spending. While it's natural to enjoy the fruits of your labour, it's crucial to maintain a balanced approach to avoid jeopardising your long-term financial security.

- **Sustainable Spending:** Develop a sustainable spending plan that allows you to enjoy your wealth while ensuring that you don't outlive your assets. A common guideline is the "4% rule," which suggests that you can safely withdraw 4% of your portfolio's value each year in retirement without depleting your principal. However, this is just a rule of thumb, and your individual circumstances may require a different approach.

- **Mindful Consumption:** Avoid the trap of lifestyle inflation, where your spending increases in lockstep with your income or wealth. Be mindful of your consumption habits and focus on experiences and purchases that bring you genuine value and happiness. Differentiate between needs and wants, and avoid unnecessary expenses that can erode your wealth over time.

- **Giving Back:** Consider incorporating philanthropy into your financial plan. Giving back to your community or supporting causes you care about can be a rewarding way to use your wealth and make a positive impact on the world. You might choose to donate to charities, establish a foundation, or engage in impact investing, where you invest in businesses or projects that generate both financial returns and social or environmental benefits.

Having the Mindset of a Wealth Builder

Maintaining and growing wealth requires a mindset shift from wealth accumulation to wealth preservation and stewardship.

- **Long-Term Perspective:** Continue to focus on your long-term financial goals, even as your wealth grows. Avoid making impulsive decisions based on short-term market fluctuations or emotional factors. Remember that your financial journey is a marathon, not a sprint, and that patience and discipline are still essential.

- **Continuous Learning:** Stay informed about economic trends, investment strategies, and changes in tax laws. The financial landscape is constantly evolving, and continuous learning is crucial to making informed decisions. Read books, attend seminars, follow reputable financial news sources, and consider seeking ongoing advice from qualified professionals.

- **Professional Guidance:** As your wealth grows, the complexity of your financial situation may increase. Consider working with a team of trusted advisors, including a financial planner, tax advisor, estate planning attorney, and potentially an investment manager. These professionals can provide expert guidance and help you navigate the challenges and opportunities that come with significant wealth.

- **Legacy Planning:** Think about the legacy you want to leave behind. This might involve passing on your wealth to future generations, supporting charitable causes, or making a lasting impact on your community. Engaging in thoughtful legacy planning can provide a sense of purpose and ensure that your wealth is used in a way that aligns with your values.

What if I do not possess any other skills?

The world is a harsh place with very stiff competition. Even if you secure a decent job now, it doesn't guarantee that you will be able to retain that job forever. The company might replace you with someone cheaper but with better skills than you if you remained stagnant without being able to provide any additional value to the company. Therefore, it is wiser to pick up a new skill that is in high demand or advance your current skill sets to remain relevant in the job industry. I have seen many who have gotten too comfortable at their job where they are not bothered to learn new things. When a new manager or a CEO took over the company, they were on the top of the list for termination.

Acquiring new skills or learning new things would also help you to relook and rethink about your future. You will be able to try out new jobs that you never knew you could be so passionate about. You could be having that creative and artistic mind locked away deep inside you. On the exterior, you are a programmer doing the mundane coding tasks every day. You did not have the chance to display your creative side because you were asked to follow and code according to the design given by your supervisor.

Turning Your Skills into Side Hustle Gold

In today's dynamic economy, relying solely on a single source of income can be precarious. Exploring skills to create a side hustle and generate income is a great way to diversify your income streams, leverage your talents, and build a more secure financial future. A side hustle can be your safety net, your creative outlet, and your pathway to financial freedom. It's about taking control of your earning potential and building something of your own. Here's a step-by-step guide on how you can transform your existing skills or cultivate new ones into a thriving side hustle:

Assess Your Current Skills and Interests

The foundation of any successful side hustle lies in identifying your strengths, passions, and existing skill sets. These can come from your professional experiences, hobbies, or even just the things you enjoy doing in your free time. Don't underestimate the value of seemingly "ordinary" skills; what comes naturally to you might be highly sought after by others. This is about taking an inventory of your personal assets.

- **Create a Skills Inventory:** Dedicate some time to brainstorming and creating a comprehensive list of your skills. Think broadly and include everything, no matter how insignificant it may seem. Consider technical skills (e.g., coding, writing, design), soft skills (e.g., communication, organisation, problem-solving), creative skills (e.g., photography, music, crafting), and even knowledge-based skills (e.g., expertise in a particular subject, industry knowledge).

- **Identify Your Passions:** What do you love to do? What activities make you lose track of time? Your passions are a great source of potential side hustle ideas because you're more likely to stay motivated and engaged if you enjoy what you're doing.

- **Reflect on Your Experiences:** Think about your past professional and personal experiences. What tasks did you excel at? What did you enjoy the most? What kind of feedback did you receive from others?

- **Ask for Feedback:** Sometimes it's hard to see our own strengths. Reach out to friends, family, colleagues, or mentors and ask them what they think you're good at. You might be surprised by their insights.

- **Categorise Your Skills:** Once you have a list, try to categorise your skills. This will make it easier to identify potential side hustle opportunities. For example, you might group skills under headings like "Writing & Communication," "Design & Creative," "Technical & IT," "Business & Marketing," etc.

- **Analyse your spare time**: Evaluate your hobbies, interests, and activities you engage in during your free time. What do you find yourself doing when you're not working or fulfilling other obligations? This can reveal hidden talents or passions that you could potentially monetise.

- **Consider your knowledge base**: Reflect on your educational background, specialised training, or areas of expertise. What do you know a lot about? This could be anything from history to gardening to astrophysics. Your knowledge can be a valuable asset in creating a side hustle.

Questions to Ask Yourself:

- What am I consistently praised for?
- What tasks do I find easy that others find challenging?
- What do I enjoy doing in my spare time, even if I'm not getting paid for it?
- What skills or knowledge do I have that others might find valuable and be willing to pay for?
- What are my core values, and what kind of work aligns with them?
- What problems do I enjoy solving?
- What are some things I've always wanted to learn or try?

Example:

Let's say you're a web developer. Your technical skills might include coding languages like HTML, CSS, JavaScript, and Python. You might also have experience with website design, UX/UI principles, and database management. Perhaps you enjoy photography as a hobby, and you're particularly good at photo editing. You might also be a skilled communicator, able to explain complex technical concepts in a clear and concise way. All these skills could potentially be turned into a side hustle. You could consider any of the following: freelance web development, creating and selling stock photography, offering photo editing services, or even teaching online courses on web development or photography.

Research Market Demand

Once you have a good understanding of your skills and interests, it's crucial to research whether there's a market demand for them. Some skills are in high demand for side hustles, while others may require you to build an audience or carve out a specific niche. You need to determine if people are willing to pay for what you have to offer. This is where you validate your idea.

- **Explore Freelance Marketplaces:** Websites like Upwork, Fiverr, and Freelancer are great places to see what services are in demand. Browse through the categories and look for skills that match yours. Pay attention to the number of freelancers offering similar services, the rates they charge, and the number of jobs posted.

- **Use Keyword Research Tools:** Tools like Google Keyword Planner, Ahrefs, and Semrush can help you understand how many people are searching for specific keywords related to your skills or services. This can give you an idea of the potential market size.

- **Analyse Google Trends:** Google Trends allows you to see how the popularity of search terms changes over time. This can help you identify emerging trends and see if the demand for your skills is growing or declining.

- **Check Social Media and Online Communities:** Look for Facebook groups, Reddit threads, or LinkedIn discussions related to your skills or industry. See what people are talking about, what questions they're asking, and what problems they're trying to solve. This can give you valuable insights into the market demand.

- **Study Competitor Analysis:** Identify individuals or businesses offering similar services or products. Analyse their pricing, marketing strategies, and customer reviews. This will help you understand the competitive landscape and identify opportunities to differentiate yourself.

- **Identify your target audience**: Who are the people or businesses that would benefit from your skills or services? Understanding your target audience will help you tailor your offerings and marketing efforts.

- **Validate your idea**: Before investing too much time and effort, validate your idea by talking to potential customers. Get feedback on your offerings and see if there's genuine interest.

Example:

Continuing with our web developer example, you might find that there's a high demand for freelance web developers on Upwork, particularly those with experience in e-commerce platforms like Shopify. You might also discover that there's a growing trend for website accessibility audits, which is something you could specialise in. On social media, you might find businesses complaining about slow website loading times, indicating a need for website optimisation services.

Learn New Skills

If you identify a skill that has strong market potential but you're not yet proficient in it, consider investing time in learning or improving that skill. The good news is that there are countless resources available online, both free and paid, to help you acquire new skills or enhance existing ones. This is where you invest in yourself.

- **Identify Skill Gaps:** Based on your market research, pinpoint the specific skills that are in high demand but are not yet part of your repertoire. Be honest about your current skill level and identify areas where you need to improve.

- **Explore Free Resources:** Start with free online resources like YouTube tutorials, podcasts, blog posts, and articles. These can provide a good foundation and help you decide if you want to pursue a skill further.

- **Consider Paid Courses:** If you're serious about mastering a skill, consider investing in paid online courses from platforms like Skillshare, Coursera, Udemy, or LinkedIn Learning. These courses often offer more structured learning, expert instruction, and practical exercises.

- **Seek Out Certifications:** For certain skills, such as digital marketing, project management, or specific software proficiencies, obtaining industry-recognised certifications can enhance your credibility and marketability.

- **Practice Consistently:** Learning a new skill requires consistent practice. Set aside dedicated time each day or week to work on your new skill. The more you practice, the faster you'll improve.

- **Find a mentor or join a community**: Connecting with others who are learning or have mastered the skill can provide valuable support, guidance, and feedback.

- **Stay updated**: Technology and market trends are constantly evolving. Make sure to stay updated on the latest developments in your field by following industry blogs, attending webinars, or taking refresher courses.

Example:

Let's say your research indicates a high demand for mobile app developers, but you only have experience in web development. You could start by watching free YouTube tutorials on mobile app development frameworks like React Native or Flutter. If you find it interesting, you might then enrol in a paid online course on Udemy to gain a deeper understanding. You could also join online communities of mobile app developers to learn from others and get feedback on your projects.

Test Your Idea or Skill

Before fully committing to a side hustle, it's wise to test your idea or skill on a small scale to assess its potential and gather feedback. This is a crucial step to minimise risk and ensure you're on the right track. This is your Minimum Viable Product (MVP) stage.

- **Offer Services to Your Network:** Start by offering your services to friends, family, or people within your existing network. This can be a low-pressure way to gain experience, build your portfolio, and get initial testimonials.

- **Pro Bono or Discounted Work:** Consider doing pro bono (free) work or offering discounted rates initially. This can help you attract your first few clients and build a reputation.

- **Create a Prototype or MVP:** If you're developing a product or digital service, create a prototype or a Minimum Viable Product (MVP)—a basic version with just enough features to attract early-adopter customers and validate your idea.

- **Gather Feedback:** Actively seek feedback from your initial clients or users. Ask them what they liked, what they didn't like, and what could be improved. This feedback is invaluable for refining your offering.

- **Pilot Test:** If you're planning to offer a service that involves a longer-term commitment (e.g., coaching, consulting), consider running a pilot test with a small group of clients before launching it officially.

- **A/B testing**: Experiment with different approaches to your service or product. For example, if you're offering web design services, try different design styles or pricing models to see what resonates best with your target audience.

- **Iterate and refine**: Based on the feedback you receive, iterate and refine your offerings. This may involve adjusting your pricing, modifying your service delivery, or even pivoting to a slightly different niche.

Example:

As a budding web developer, you might offer to build a simple website for a friend's small business at a discounted rate. You could use this project to showcase your skills, get feedback on your process, and gather a testimonial for your portfolio. If you're developing a productivity app, you might create a basic version with limited features and release it to a small group of beta testers to gather feedback before developing the full version.

Choose a Side Hustle Model

There are numerous ways to turn your skills into income. The best model for you will depend on your goals, lifestyle, time commitment, and the nature of your skills. This is where you decide how you will operate your business.

1. Freelancing

Freelancing involves offering your services to clients on a project-by-project basis. You have the flexibility to choose your clients, projects, and working hours.

- Writing, editing, and content creation (e.g., blog posts, articles, website copy, social media content, copywriting)
- Graphic design, web design, and UX/UI design
- Social media management, digital marketing (e.g., SEO, PPC, email marketing)

- Virtual assistance, project management, administrative support
- Software development, web development, app development, IT support
- Translation and interpretation
- Video editing and animation
- Photography and photo editing
- Online tutoring and teaching

Pros: Flexibility, control over your work, potential to earn high rates.

Cons: Inconsistent income, need to constantly market yourself, responsibility for finding clients.

b. Selling Products or Digital Goods

If you have a knack for creating tangible or digital products, you can sell them online through various platforms.

- Handmade crafts, jewellery, art, clothing, and other physical goods sold on platforms like Etsy, Shopify, or Amazon Handmade.
- Digital products like e-books, online courses, printables, stock photos, design templates, software, or music.
- Print-on-demand (POD) products like t-shirts, mugs, and phone cases, where you create the designs, and a third-party company handles printing and shipping.

Pros: Potential for passive income, scalability, creative control.

Cons: Requires upfront investment (especially for physical products), marketing and sales effort, and competition.

c. Online Teaching or Coaching

If you have expertise in a particular area, you can share your knowledge and skills by teaching or coaching others online.

- Examples:
    - Tutoring students in academic subjects or test preparation.
    - Creating and selling online courses on platforms like Teachable, Udemy, or Skillshare.
    - Offering one-on-one or group coaching sessions in areas like personal development, career, fitness, or business.

Pros: Leverage your expertise, make a positive impact on others, and have the potential for recurring income.

Cons: Requires strong communication skills, marketing effort to attract students or clients, and time commitment for creating course materials or conducting coaching sessions.

d. Content Creation

If you enjoy creating engaging content, you can build an audience and monetise your content through various channels.

- Starting a YouTube channel or TikTok account and monetising through ads, sponsorships, or merchandise.

- Blogging and monetising through display advertising, affiliate marketing, sponsored content, or selling your own products or services.
- Building a large following on Instagram or Pinterest and partnering with brands for sponsored posts or affiliate marketing.
- Podcasting on a niche topic and monetising through sponsorships, advertising, or listener donations.

Pros: Creative outlet, potential to reach a large audience, multiple monetisation options.

Cons: Requires consistent effort to create high-quality content; building an audience takes time; income can be unpredictable.

e. Affiliate Marketing

Affiliate marketing involves promoting other companies' products or services and earning a commission for each sale made through your unique referral link.

- **How it Works:** You sign up for an affiliate program, get a unique link to promote, and earn a percentage of each sale made through that link.

Pros: Low barrier to entry, potential for passive income, can be combined with other side hustle models.

Cons: Requires an audience or traffic source; income depends on sales; can take time to see significant earnings.

f. Real Estate Investment or Rental Income

If you have capital to invest, real estate can be a way to generate passive income through rental properties or other investment strategies.

- Renting out a spare room, apartment, or entire property on platforms like Airbnb.
- Investing in rental properties and managing them yourself or hiring a property management company.
- Investing in Real Estate Investment Trusts (REITs) for a more passive approach.
- Flipping houses (buying, renovating, and reselling properties for a profit).
- Investing in real estate crowdfunding platforms.

Pros: Potential for high returns, passive income stream, long-term appreciation.

Cons: Requires significant upfront investment, potential for vacancies or property damage, requires knowledge of the real estate market.

Create a Business Plan or Strategy

Once you've chosen your side hustle model, it's essential to create a basic business plan or strategy. This doesn't need to be a formal, multi-page document, but it should outline your goals, target market, marketing plan, and financial projections. This is your roadmap to success.

- **Define Your Goals:** What do you want to achieve with your side hustle? Be specific about your financial goals (e.g., earn an extra $500 per month) and other objectives (e.g., gain experience in a new field, build a portfolio, etc.).

- **Identify Your Target Market:** Who are your ideal clients or customers? What are their needs, preferences, and pain points? The more specific you can be, the better you can tailor your offerings and marketing messages.

- **Develop a Marketing Plan:** How will you reach your target market? Will you use social media, paid advertising, content marketing, email marketing, networking, or a combination of strategies?

- **Create a Pricing Strategy:** How much will you charge for your services or products? Research competitor pricing and consider your costs, time, and the value you provide.

- **Outline Your Operational Plan:** How will you deliver your services or products? What tools or resources will you need? How will you manage your time and workflow?

- **Project Your Finances:** Estimate your start-up costs, ongoing expenses, and potential revenue. This will help you determine the financial viability of your side hustle.

- **Set Key Performance Indicators (KPIs):** Identify the key metrics you will track to measure your success (e.g., number of clients, website traffic, sales revenue, conversion rates).

If you decide to start a freelance writing business, your business plan might include:

- **Goal:** Earn an extra $1,000 per month within six months.
- **Target Market:** Small businesses and startups in the tech industry.
- **Marketing Plan:** Create a professional website and portfolio, join freelance platforms like Upwork, network with potential clients on LinkedIn, and use content marketing (blogging) to attract clients.
- **Pricing Strategy:** Charge per word or per project, with rates based on industry standards and your experience level.
- **Operational Plan:** Use project management software to track deadlines and client communication; invest in a good quality laptop and writing software.
- **Financial Projections:** Estimate your start-up costs (website hosting, software) and project your monthly revenue based on your target client base and pricing.
- **KPIs:** Track the number of clients acquired, average project value, website traffic, and client satisfaction ratings.

Start Small, Iterate, and Scale

It's tempting to go all-in from the start, but it's often wiser to start small, test your ideas, gather feedback, and then gradually scale your side hustle. This approach minimises risk and allows you to learn and adapt along the way. This is where you put your plan into action and refine it as you go.

- **Start with a Minimum Viable Product (MVP):** If you're developing a product or service, start with a basic version that has just enough features to attract early adopters. This allows you to test the market and gather feedback before investing too much time and resources.

- **Launch with a Small Pilot Group:** If you're offering a service, start with a small group of clients or customers. This allows you to refine your processes, identify any issues, and gather testimonials before expanding.

- **Gather Feedback and Iterate:** Actively seek feedback from your clients or customers. Use their input to improve your offerings, adjust your pricing, or refine your marketing strategies. Be prepared to iterate and adapt based on what you learn.

- **Automate and Delegate:** As your side hustle grows, look for ways to automate tasks or delegate them to others. This will free up your time to focus on higher-value activities.

- **Scale Gradually:** Once you've validated your idea and refined your processes, you can start to scale your side hustle. This might involve taking on more clients, expanding your product line, or hiring help.

Example:

If you're launching an online course, you might start by creating a short pilot course and offering it to a small group of students at a discounted price. You can then gather feedback, improve the course content, and add more modules before launching it to a wider audience. If you're starting a freelance writing business, you might start by taking on one or two small projects to build your portfolio and gain experience before pitching to larger clients.

Network and Leverage Connections

Networking is crucial for growing your side hustle, especially in the early stages. Building relationships with other professionals, potential clients, and people in your industry can open doors to new opportunities, referrals, and valuable insights. This is your support system and your source of new opportunities.

- **Join Online Communities:** Participate in online forums, Facebook groups, LinkedIn groups, and subreddits related to your industry or niche. Share your expertise, answer questions, and connect with others.

- **Attend Industry Events:** Attend virtual or in-person conferences, workshops, and meet-ups related to your field. This is a great way to meet potential clients, partners, and mentors.

- **Connect with Influencers:** Identify key influencers in your industry and engage with their content on social media. Build relationships with them by sharing their work, leaving thoughtful comments, and offering your expertise.

- **Reach Out to Potential Clients:** Don't be afraid to reach out to potential clients directly, especially if you have a targeted list. Personalise your outreach and focus on how you can help them achieve their goals.

- **Leverage Your Existing Network:** Let your friends, family, and former colleagues know about your side hustle. They might be able to refer you to potential clients or offer valuable advice.

- **Collaborate with others**: Partner with other businesses or freelancers to offer complementary services or reach a wider audience.

- **Build relationships**: Focus on building genuine relationships with people in your network. Offer help and support to others, and don't be afraid to ask for help when you need it.

Example:

If you're a freelance graphic designer, you might join online communities for designers, attend local design meet-ups, and connect with marketing professionals on LinkedIn. You could also reach out to small businesses in your area and offer your services. If you're starting a fitness coaching business, you might connect with local gyms or fitness studios to explore potential partnerships.

Section 9: Stay Consistent and Adapt

Building a successful side hustle takes time, effort, and persistence. It's not a get-rich-quick scheme. You need to be prepared to put in the work, stay consistent, and adapt to changing circumstances. This is where your dedication and resilience will be tested.

Building a profitable and sustainable side hustle is a marathon, not a sprint.

- **Set Realistic Goals:** Begin with achievable goals for your side hustle, both short-term and long-term. This will help you stay motivated and track your progress. Don't try to do too much too soon. Start with small, manageable goals that you can realistically achieve, and gradually increase the scope and complexity of your side hustle as you gain experience and confidence.

- **Create a Schedule:** Dedicate specific time slots each day or week to work on your side hustle. Treat it like a real job, even if it's just for a few hours. Consistency is key to making progress. Block out time in your calendar and stick to your schedule as much as possible. This will help you develop a routine and make your side hustle a regular part of your life.

- **Stay Organised:** Use project management tools, calendars, and to-do lists to stay organised and manage your time effectively. This is especially important when juggling a side hustle with other commitments. There are many free and paid tools available to help you manage your tasks, deadlines, and client communications.

- **Track Your Progress:** Regularly monitor your key performance indicators (KPIs) to see how your side hustle is performing. This will help you identify areas where you're doing well and areas where you need to improve. Track your income, expenses, website traffic, social media engagement, or any other metrics that are relevant to your side hustle.

- **Learn from Your Mistakes:** Don't be afraid to make mistakes. They are inevitable. The important thing is to learn from them and use those lessons to improve your side hustle. Every mistake is an opportunity to learn and grow. Analyse what went wrong, identify areas for improvement, and adjust your strategy accordingly.

- **Stay Up-to-Date:** The world of side hustles is constantly evolving. Keep learning and stay updated on the latest trends, technologies, and best practices in your industry. This will help you stay competitive and offer the best possible services or products. Subscribe to industry blogs, follow relevant social media accounts, attend webinars or online courses, and network with other professionals in your field.

- **Adapt to Change:** Be prepared to adapt your side hustle to changing market conditions, customer feedback, and new opportunities. The ability to pivot and evolve is crucial for long-term success. Don't be afraid to experiment with new ideas, try different approaches, and adjust your strategy as needed. The most successful side hustles are those that can adapt to the ever-changing needs of the market.
- **Celebrate Your Successes:** Acknowledge and celebrate your achievements along the way, no matter how small. This will help you stay motivated and maintain a positive outlook. Rewarding yourself for your hard work will

reinforce positive habits and keep you energised on your journey.

- **Don't Give Up:** There will be times when you feel discouraged or overwhelmed. Remember why you started your side hustle in the first place and keep pushing forward. Persistence is key to achieving your goals. Building a successful side hustle takes time and effort. Don't expect to see results overnight. Stay focused on your vision, and don't let setbacks derail you.

Side Hustle Ideas Based on Common Skills

To help you brainstorm, here's a list of side hustle ideas based on common skills. This is not an exhaustive list, but it can serve as a starting point for your own exploration.

Writing & Communication:

- Freelance writing (blog posts, articles, website copy, etc.)
- Copywriting (sales pages, email sequences, ad copy)
- Editing and proofreading
- Content creation (social media content, video scripts)
- Blogging
- eBook writing and publishing
- Technical writing
- Resume and cover letter writing
- Translation services

Design & Creative:

- Graphic design (logos, brochures, marketing materials)
- Web design
- UX/UI design
- Illustration
- Photography (stock photography, event photography, portrait photography)
- Photo editing and retouching
- Video editing and animation
- Handmade crafts (jewellery, candles, soaps, etc.)
- Interior design consulting

Technical & IT:

- Web development
- App development
- Software development
- IT support and troubleshooting
- Data entry and management
- Website maintenance and security
- Coding tutor

Business & Marketing:

- Social media management
- Digital marketing (SEO, PPC, email marketing)
- Virtual assistant services
- Project management
- Market research and analysis
- Business plan writing
- Consulting (in your area of expertise)
- Bookkeeping

Teaching & Coaching:

- Online tutoring (academic subjects, test prep)
- Language tutoring
- Music lessons
- Fitness training and coaching
- Life coaching
- Career coaching
- Online course creation

Others:

- Event planning
- Personal shopping
- Pet sitting or dog walking
- House cleaning or organising
- Delivery services (food, groceries)
- Ride-sharing (Uber, Lyft)
- Real estate investing

In the End

The journey to your first million, as you've now seen, is not paved with overnight riches or effortless victories. It is, instead, a testament to the power of hard work, unwavering dedication, discipline, and steadfast commitment. It is a journey that demands strategic planning, meticulous execution, and the resilience to weather inevitable storms.

I hoped this book has granted you some insights with the "divide and conquer" strategy, an interesting idea for treating life as a constant battle for achieving your financial goals. However, the true path to your success will always be your own relentless drive.

This strategy is not merely about accumulating wealth; it's about transforming your relationship with money, turning it from a source of anxiety into a tool for empowerment. It's about conquering your financial battlefield, not through reckless charges but through calculated manoeuvres, strategic deployment of your resources (your saving pots), and the wisdom to distinguish between treacherous landmines and valuable strongholds. The steps outlined, from eliminating bad debts to acquiring good debts and building multiple income streams, are the tactics of a savvy financial general, leading their forces to victory.

One key thing that I learnt during the journey was that the first million is not an end, but a beginning. It's a validation of the "divide and conquer" approach, a proof of concept that you can replicate and scale. It is the foundation upon which you build an even greater empire. Reaching this milestone instills a newfound confidence, a deep understanding of the principles that govern wealth creation. It is not merely about reaching a specific number; it is about adopting a mindset, a way of thinking about your finances that will serve you for the rest of your life. Now that you've tasted your first pot of success, the next stage is to replicate the steps, to apply the same principles with even greater conviction and wisdom. Your first rental property has become a stream of passive income, your first successful investment has boosted your confidence in navigating the stock market, and your first side hustle has proven your ability to generate income beyond your primary job. Now is the time to multiply those successes, to create the next rental property income stream, your next investment, and your next side hustle. This will allow you to quickly replicate your first pot of success.

This is not simply about repeating the same actions; it's about leveraging the knowledge and experience you've gained. You now have a deeper understanding of your own strengths and weaknesses, a clearer vision of your financial goals, and a more refined strategy for achieving them. Your subsequent ventures will benefit from the lessons learnt, the mistakes avoided, and the successes celebrated. As you progress, the challenges will inevitably become more complex, the stakes higher, and the risks more pronounced. The financial battlefield will continue to evolve, presenting new obstacles and demanding greater adaptability. You might encounter more sophisticated "booby traps" in the form of tempting but ultimately unprofitable investments. You might face periods of economic uncertainty that require adjustments to your strategy. You may even choose to try out various methods along the way. For each method, you will be analysing the results, comparing them, and refining your approach. This iterative process of testing, learning, and adjusting is crucial for continuous improvement.

This is where your commitment to continuous learning becomes even more critical. The financial landscape is constantly changing, and staying ahead of the curve requires a dedication to expanding your knowledge, seeking out new opportunities, and refining your understanding of market dynamics. It's about embracing a growth mindset, viewing challenges not as roadblocks but as opportunities for learning and improvement. The "divide and conquer" strategy provides a robust framework, but it is not a rigid formula. It's a flexible approach that must be adapted to your unique circumstances, evolving goals, and the ever-changing realities of the financial world. Learn from each experience, adjust your formula, and keep moving forward.

Your financial journey does not end at one million; it is merely a significant milestone. You have proven that you have the discipline, the knowledge, and the resilience to achieve remarkable things. Now, armed with the wisdom gained from your initial success, you are ready to scale new heights, to build an even more prosperous and secure financial future, an empire that will stand the test of time. The journey continues, and the next million awaits. The key is to keep dividing, keep conquering, and keep building, one strategic step at a time. It is to keep reinvesting into your saving pots, keep acquiring strategic strongholds, and constantly learning from the battles you have fought. Your journey to financial freedom is not a sprint to the finish line but a lifelong marathon. Embrace the challenges, celebrate the victories, and never lose sight of the empire you are building, an empire built not just on wealth but on the unshakeable foundation of your own financial wisdom. You are no longer just conquering the financial battlefield.

You will need to manage it, defend it, and make sure that it will last for generations to come.

Wishing you abundant blessings as you journey towards a achieving your financial freedom and goals!

Copyright © 2024 Benjamin M.

All rights reserved. No content of this book may be reproduced and republished in any form and in any means without the permission in writing from the author of this book.

www.ingramcontent.com/pod-product-compliance
Lightning Source LLC
Chambersburg PA
CBHW050311230526
45471CB00005B/2118